Civil War Stories

Georgia Southern University

Jack N. and Addie D. Averitt Lecture Series

No. 7

Civil War Stories

Catherine Clinton

The University of Georgia Press | Athens and London

Athens, Georgia 30602

Designed by Kathi Morgan

Set in New Caledonia by G&S Typesetters, Inc.

Printed and bound by Maple-Vail Book Manufacturing Group

The paper in this book meets the guidelines for permanence and durability of the Committee on Production Guidelines for Book Longevity of the Council on Library Resources.

Printed in the United States of America

02 01 00 99 98 C 5 4 3 2 1

LIBRARY OF CONGRESS CATALOGING IN PUBLICATION DATA

Clinton, Catherine, 1952–

Civil War stories / Catherine Clinton.

p. cm. — (Jack N. and Addie D. Averitt lecture series ; no. 7)

Includes bibliographical references and index.

ISBN 0-8203-2028-5 (alk. paper); 0-8203-2074-9 (pbk.: alk. paper)

1. United States—History—Civil War, 1861–1865—Social aspects—Anecdotes. 2. United States—History—Civil War, 1861–1865—Psychological aspects—Anecdotes. 3. United States—History—Civil War, 1861–1865—Women—Anecdotes. 4. United States—History—Civil War, 1861–1865—Children—Anecdotes. I. Title. II. Series.

E468.9.C57 1998

973.7—dc21 98-15523

BRITISH LIBRARY CATALOGING IN PUBLICATION DATA AVAILABLE

Dedicated to

Fran and Craig D'Ooge and

Tim and Caroline Clark—

hosts, storytellers, and friends extraordinaire

CONTENTS

FOREWORD

ON OCTOBER 1–2, 1996, THE HISTORY DEPARTMENT of Georgia Southern University hosted the Seventh Annual Jack N. and Addie D. Averitt Lecture Series. The speaker, Dr. Catherine Clinton of the W. E. B. Du Bois Institute of Harvard University, captivated her audiences with stories of women, men, and children caught up in the turmoil of the Civil War. Subsequently, she expanded the original lectures into the essays presented in this volume.

Professor Clinton is recognized as a leading scholar in the fields of southern history and American women's history. Since the publication of her first book, *The Plantation Mistress: Woman's World in the Old South,* in 1982, she has been a prolific writer and editor, producing numerous articles and books. As the seventh lecturer in the Averitt series, Clinton joined the distinguished historians and literary critics—Eugene D. Genovese, James Olney, George B. Tindall, Tony Tanner, Samuel S. Hill, and Barbara Hardy—who have presented the lectures in years past.

When she accepted the invitation to deliver the Averitt Lectures, Professor Clinton promised to ground her presentations in stories that illustrated the human dimensions of the Civil War. She kept her word. In these essays Clinton recounts the experiences of individuals and families whose lives were transformed by war. She interweaves discussions of well-known historical figures, such as Clara Barton and Rose Greenhow, with accounts of other lesser-known people, like Frances Rollin and Louisa McCord Smythe, whose names are absent from most history textbooks. Delineating the characters of people who displayed an array of strengths and weaknesses, Clinton shares compelling tales of fear and courage, love and heartache, jealousy and forgiveness. Set against the backdrop of the bloodiest war in American history, the emotions and personal conflicts portrayed in *Civil War Stories* will resonate with contemporary audiences.

The essays remind us that narrative is at the heart of the historian's craft, but this book is more than a random collection of anecdotes from the past. Clinton uses these stories to explore recent themes in historical scholarship and to offer new directions for future research. She examines the impact of the Civil War on civilians within frameworks established by historians of women and gender. In the first essay, Clinton shows how politics invaded the sanctity of the home and approaches a familiar theme from a different angle, presenting the sectional crisis as a conflict that created rifts between women on the home front at the same time that it pitted brother against brother on the battlefield. In the second, she charts newly discovered historical terrain, suggesting that scholars study the experiences of the vast numbers of children orphaned by the war. In the final chapter, she contributes to the burgeoning interest in the creation of historical memory, contrasting the ways in which whites and African Americans in post-Reconstruction South Carolina remembered the Old South and interpreted the Civil War. Throughout the book, Clinton offers a unique perspective on one of the most closely scrutinized periods in American history.

Many people worked to make these lectures possible. First and foremost, thanks are extended to Dr. and Mrs. Averitt, who endowed the series in 1990. Their generous gift is just one of the many tangible and intangible contributions they have made to enrich the lives of people on the Georgia Southern campus and in the Statesboro community. Former and current chairs of the department of history, Dr. Walter J. Fraser Jr. and Dr. Jerome O. Steffen, along with University President Dr. Nicholas Henry and Vice President for Academic Affairs Dr. Harry Carter, have been enthusiastic supporters of the series. Members of the Averitt Lecture Series Committee—co-chairs Dr. Alan C. Downs, Dr. Ruth A. Thompson, and Dr. George H. Shriver—were efficient and cooperative. Ms. Pat Lanier and Ms. Lisa Sapp, secretaries in the department of history, deserve special thanks for cheerfully assuming additional responsibilities during one of the busiest times of the academic year. Mr. Malcolm Call of the University of Georgia Press continues to offer valuable advice and assistance. Finally, thanks to two former members of the committee, Dr. R. Frank Saunders Jr. and Ms. Esther Mallard. They established a tradition of excellence for the lecture series and generously shared the expertise gained from experience with the current committee.

Anastatia Sims
Co-chair, Averitt Lecture Series Committee

CHAPTER ONE

Sister against Sister

Fanny Kemble's Divided Daughters

SEVERAL GENERATIONS OF AMERICAN HISTORIANS have debated the events leading up to the Civil War, creating layer upon layer of argument, building a mountain of scholarship that defies summary. So much so that I often wonder, while wading through citations and CD-ROMs and World Wide Web pages, what am I expecting to find? What is left to plumb? Why do we scholars persist with our endless rhetoric and research?

Because the Civil War calls each rising generation to plunge back in time and explore this great gaping wound in our body politic, to discuss and dispute this dramatic dimension of our glorious and grievous past. How and why hundreds upon thousands died is outranked only by data on who and where they perished. The human face of Civil War studies has shifted from the stoic triptych of Lee, Davis, and Jackson—even beyond the wan visage of Lincoln or the gleaming monuments to generals on horseback—to the everyday and extraordinary people who participated: the black corporal with the Fifty-fourth Massachusetts who wrote letters home from the battlefront;[1] the immigrant soldiers and runaway farmboys; the sutler and smugglers; the girl who disguised herself as a man, donned a uniform, and died a soldier.[2] Also stoic mothers and abandoned sweethearts, divided families, and thousands of displaced refugees whose letters poured forth are finally being given their place in the publishing enterprise, as recaptured voices of the struggle, eyewitness to triumph and tragedy, lives forever marked by war.

Now we can put many more faces on the war, especially in the wake of Ken Burns's successful PBS series *The Civil War*, first broadcast in 1990. The characterization of the Civil War as a "brother's war" underscores the universality of this bloody strife, even as it perhaps diminishes the war's wider impact when viewed only as some sort of family squabble within our past rather than the "Second American Revolution" or a "war for black liberation" or a moment in time when the future of the entire Continent, and even the destiny of the hemisphere, would hang in the balance. Of course, it can be all of this and more, as it was for Americans who witnessed it and those who heard about it for generations to come.

The family metaphor appeals, especially to social historians seeking to engage an audience outside the academy. What greater intrigue than imagining one family member facing another, siblings in the rifle sight. But also in vogue is an awareness that all wars are not won or lost simply when armies meet in combat. Sherman himself taught the politicians about breaking the rebellion by going after civilians, crushing the countryside with the hard hand of war.[3] A combination of factors on the home front turned the tide, as crucial to the final outcome as military strategy and body counts.[4]

More and more we are interested in learning not just statistics and official records but the stories of war—the true and even embellished tales offering a human scale. By telling these "stories," we historians can abandon the tricks of the trade and provide a series of interconnected images of people and events that together paint a portrait, a narrative "moving picture." It is a hard lesson to learn, but being a southern historian, I am grateful for the luxury of a southern audience that has more than once reminded me—without a story it's all just words.

To that end, I would like to share the saga of one intriguing family's civil war. There are many different ways I could have outlined the cast of characters and their conflicts, but I have chosen "Sister against Sister."[5] The name of Fanny Kemble is widely known in nineteenth-century Anglo-American circles, and her plantation journal is well known—or infamous. But her daughters are another story, a story within a story that I will recount in abbreviated form.[6]

Fanny Kemble was born in London in 1809 into the first family of the London stage. Despite her royal theatrical lineage (the niece of John Kemble and Sarah Siddons, the daughter of Charles Kemble), her parents' household always seemed in a state of imminent financial disaster. Fanny's parents managed to send her to a finishing school in Paris, but the Kembles' financial turmoil continued throughout Fanny's formative years. After the end of her formal education, she enjoyed her older brother John's literary friends from Cambridge, known as the Apostles (William Makepeace Thackeray and other luminaries), and began to write plays. When foreclosure threatened her father's theater, Covent Garden, Fanny's desperate parents staged her theatrical debut in the title role of Shakespeare's Juliet in October 1829—and her stage career was launched.

She became an overnight sensation—wined and dined and treated as the new star in the firmament. Despite all this lavish attention, Kemble was not enamored of a life on the boards, believing "acting has always appeared to be the very lowest of the arts, admitting that it deserves to be classed among them at all, which I am not sure it does."[7] In spite of her misgivings, she played to packed houses, and with the revenues rolling in, lifted her family out of dire economic straits. In 1831 she appeared in one of her own plays, a novelty at the time, quite remarkable for a woman. This minor literary coup allowed her to dream of escaping the stage to become a writer. Although she aspired to become a great writer, her career as an actress, she later confessed, "minted" her money.

Despite Fanny's success, Charles Kemble announced that a two year tour of States was the only solution to settle family debts—a plan to which Fanny only reluctantly consented. Setting sail for a prolonged absence from home was softened for Fanny when she and her father were accompanied by her Aunt Adelaide, known as Dall, the person to whom Fanny was closest, and who would serve as her niece's chaperone, dresser, and confidante.

American audiences claimed to have never seen Kemble's equal. Fanny was inundated with flowers, demands for interviews from reporters, and followed by a drove of adoring suitors. She enjoyed her celebrity but was bored by most of her admirers. She did take some interest in some of the bluestocking women she encountered and became fast friends with the Massachusetts writer Catharine Sedgwick and, eventually, Sedgwick's entire Brahmin clan.

During her visit to Philadelphia, Kemble commented: "I like this place better than New York; it has an air of greater age. It has altogether a rather dull, sober, mellow hue which is more agreeable than the glaring newness of New York."[8] In Philadelphia, Fanny Kemble met her future husband, Pierce Butler.

Butler derived his social position, eventual wealth, and even his surname from his mother's family. Pierce and his brother John secured a fortune by changing their last name from Mease to Butler in order to inherit from their grandfather, Major Pierce Butler. The bulk of the Major's holdings, slaves and other properties (including dower from his wife's family, the Middletons of South Carolina), remained in the hands of his daughters. The Major had cut his son Thomas out of the will when he married a French woman to whom the Major objected, and indeed he disinherited Thomas's children. Al-

Fanny Kemble during her twenties.
Courtesy of the Coastal Georgia Historical Society.

though Major Butler gave his sole surviving son some lavish gifts, such as a home in Philadelphia, the bulk of his fortune went to other male heirs, his grandsons by his daughter Sarah. The Mease brothers, once they became Butlers, looked forward to wealth and social status, derived from the Major's largesse. Pierce especially never entertained any idea of employment.

Once he changed his name at the age of sixteen, he became Pierce Butler. And he had to change both names: christened Pierce Butler Mease, he was originally called Butler Mease, and not wanting to be called "Butler Butler," he had to take both a new surname and first name. As a young man he enjoyed playing the flute, attending costume balls, and other diversions of high society. When Kemble debuted in Philadelphia, Butler secured a letter of introduction. The meeting was much more momentous for Butler, who was obviously smitten and hoped to elicit some spark of passion, which was not forthcoming at the outset. After being love struck, Butler followed Kemble up and down the East Coast, often playing in the orchestra pit during her performances. Kemble was clearly flattered and amused but not in any way enthralled.

Butler was persistent and, by the time he wanted to marry Fanny, rumors were flying on both sides of the Atlantic about the couple. There was no small discouragement of the liaison from the Sedgwicks. Catharine Sedgwick voiced "a thousand fears" for the pair, as Butler was "so infinitely inferior to her that the experiment of marriage might be dangerous."[9] Charles Kemble was in no hurry to see his gold mine married off, even to a wealthy American. When a favorite cousin of Fanny's, Cecilia Siddons, wed in September 1833, Fanny's pleasure was perhaps tinged with envy. When her aunt Dall fell ill in the winter of 1833–34, debilitated as a result of a coach accident, the doctor predicted she would remain an invalid if she survived her illness. Fanny nursed her sick aunt by day, performing with her father by night.

In a fit of desperation, Fanny agreed to sell the private journal of her travels in America after being offered a substantial sum by an American publisher. She hoped this money could provide an annuity for her debilitated aunt, but shortly after signing the contract Fanny reported: "Dear Dall has gone from us. . . . She died in my arms. . . . I have almost cried my eyes out daily for the last three months. . . . I am working again, and go about my work feeling stunned and bewildered."[10] Kemble sought comfort from Butler, and shortly thereafter they were married.

Clearly, Fanny's distraught mood contributed to her decision to abandon her stage career and wed. Despite her friends' fears and her parents' opposition, Kemble insisted upon accepting Butler's offer. A Mr. Hodgkinson, whom Kemble met on the Atlantic crossing, "showed his regard by endeavoring to make [Kemble's] aunt and father aware of Mr. Butler's character " and "cautions reached [Kemble] at second hand through [her] aunt." Fanny further confessed that Hodgkinson spoke "guardedly and generally, tho' I suppose he knew much of Mr. Butler's early career of profligacy, but I was in 'love and pleased with him' and paid little heed."[11] Fanny Kemble ignored all storm warnings, marrying Butler despite several severe reservations on the part of trusted friends.

Kemble hoped marriage would allow her to retire from the stage, to devote herself to her writing, to escape the rigors of her theatrical duties. Only the acquisition of a husband could extricate her from responsibilities as the Kemble meal ticket. However, Fanny tried to please everyone and wrote to a friend on May 30, 1834, indicating she planned to return to England—as her father had already secured bookings for them. Yet she insisted that she must first marry Butler, stating: "Pierce has promised me that this shall not interfere with the discharge of my duties to my father, and relying implicitly as I do on his word, I could not resist his earnest entreaties to be his wife."[12]

The couple exchanged vows in Christ Church Philadelphia on June 7, 1834. But when it came time for Fanny to set sail for England a few days later, Pierce Butler broke his word. He convinced his bride she could not accompany her father but had to retire from acting and remain by his side. The parting between Kemble and his daughter was bitter, but only one of many obstacles the newlyweds faced.

Although Fanny later disingenuously declared she had no idea that Butler money came from slaveholding, it is clear that she had little idea about the details of her husband's financial affairs. She assumed he was well off. But in fact, once they were married, it became clear that the bulk of Butler's money was tied up in trust, until the death of his Aunt Frances, executor of the Major's estate. The couple moved into a modest and poorly maintained family estate, Butler Place, in Branchtown, six miles outside Philadelphia. When Fanny wanted to renovate, Pierce warned the property still belonged to his aunt. So Kemble was quickly disabused of the notion that she was a comfortable matron of means and became a lady-in-waiting, politely anticipating the future fortune. Equally irritating, Fanny loathed American social conventions, particularly that drawing rooms were segregated by sex after dinner and other provincialities.

In November 1834, only a few months after her marriage, Fanny Kemble wrote a farewell note, gathered her belongings, and fled the Butler home, determined to abandon her husband. The exact nature of the quarrel remains a mystery, but its melodramatic dimensions became a part of the couple's marital routine. In this initial recorded episode, the couple reunited much later on the night of her departure, but this incident reflected a pattern repeated over the next fifteen tumultuous years—quarreling, flights, and tearful reconciliation.

Kemble had promised her American diary to a publisher and was undertaking revisions. She had decided to turn over the royalties to Dall's sister, who was eking out a living as a governess in England. Further, Fanny was dead keen to resume her writing. Butler vehemently opposed Fanny's publications, especially any under her own name now that she had become his wife. Their wrangling depleted her. It took all Kemble's strength to resist Butler's opposition to continuing her writing career.

A bride less than six months, Fanny summed up her thoughts to her good friend, and divorcée, Anna Jameson: "Of course kindred, if not absolutely similar minds do exist; but they do not often meet, I think and hardly ever unite. . . . I suppose the influence of those who differ from us is more wholesome; for in mere *unison* of thought and feeling there could be no exercise for forbearance, toleration, self-examination by comparison with another nature, of the sifting of one's own opinions and feelings, and testing their accuracy and value, by contact and contrast with opposite feelings and opinions."[13] Kemble seemed to be trying to make lemonade out of the lemon with which she had been stuck.

By this time Fanny Kemble was expecting her first child. Throughout her pregnancy, Fanny was miserable and begged to be sent home to England. Butler hoped a baby would preoccupy his restless wife, but when Sarah Butler was born on May 28, 1835, Fanny's melancholy increased. She wrote to her husband in the summer,

> I am weary of my useless existence, my superintendence in your house is nominal; you have never allowed it to be otherwise; you will suffer no inconvenience from its cessation. . . . If you procure a health nurse for the baby she will not suffer; and provided she is fed, she will not fret after me. Had I died when she was born you must have taken this measure, and my parting from her now will be to her though she had never known me, and to me far less miserable than at any future time. I must beg you will take measures for my going away.[14]

She did not leave, and the couple hobbled along. Fanny Kemble was perhaps never destined to be a contented hausfrau, regardless of her mate. But Butler's relentless campaign to subdue his errant wife fueled their antagonism—not unlike Petruchio in *The Taming of the Shrew,* without the putatively happy ending.

Kemble became withdrawn and introspective. She began referring to her books as her fondest companions. She took up reviewing but not for glory, as her pieces were published anonymously, and she received no financial compensation. But she insisted she needed to write just to keep her senses keen. Kemble scribbled an impassioned political document in 1835—a "long and vehement treatise against negro slavery." Ironically, Butler's aunt, the gatekeeper of the Butler legacy, died shortly thereafter. Suddenly, Fanny was confronted by her complicity with slavery: that the comforts of her home and lifestyle were bought by slavery's filthy lucre. She wrote despondently: "Though the toilsome earnings of my daily bread were to be my lot again tomorrow, I should rejoice with unspeakable thankfulness that we had not to answer for what I consider so grievous a sin against humanity."[15]

Fanny was miserable about this new status—a slaveholder's wife—and refused to stifle her antislavery sympathies. Her vocal disdain provoked "amazement and dismay, terror and disgust" among her family and Philadelphia friends. She later confessed, "I must have appeared to them nothing but a mischievous madwoman."[16]

At the same time, these kinds of debates and divides were erupting in parlors up and down the Atlantic coast, spreading out on riverways and leapfrogging across the nation's expanding frontiers. Increasingly, attitudes toward slavery created a social litmus, a test that was total and absolute for polite society. Previously, people sidestepped the slavery issue when it arose, North and South being cemented by marital and financial ties. But by the 1830s antislavery became such a compelling cause for so many that polite society could no longer turn its head.

Many antislavery activists forged a separate aristocracy in the wake of this development. Especially within New England and Middle Atlantic urban enclaves, connections with slaveholders were spurned to keep social circles free of guilt by association. Some were eased out of high society by their impolitic insistence on preaching the sins of slavery, especially women who did not subscribe to the rigid restrictions on female behavior. Just as many reveled in their separatist status. Maria Weston Chapman of Boston was a forerunner of "abolitionist chic."[17] Included in this snobby vanguard were the several branches of the Sedgwick clan, including Fanny's closest New England friends, Charles and Elizabeth Sedgwick of Lenox, Massachusetts.

In the Winter of 1836 when Butler's supervision was required at his newly acquired Georgia estates, Fanny begged to accompany him South. Instead, he sent her to London, a bribe to keep her away from his plantations. Butler spent time in Georgia before he joined his wife and daughter in England in the Autumn of 1837. Absence allowed the couple to grow fonder, and Kemble arrived home in Pennsylvania pregnant with her second child. The following year a second daughter, Frances (nicknamed Fan), was born on her sister Sarah's third birthday. The couple experienced a rare period of harmony, until the Fall when Fanny's mother, an ocean away, fell ill and died.

Fanny was completely overwrought by the loss of her mother. Aware of her fragile state, Butler decided to allow his grieving wife to accompany him to Georgia and to bring along the children and their Irish nurse. This decision proved disastrous.

Fanny's eyewitness account of her several months in the sea islands has proven a rich and valuable resource for historians of the nineteenth-century South. Her journal chronicles many things, including the disintegration of a marriage. Butler mistakenly believed his wife's antislavery bent would be softened by contact with plantation life. He totally miscalculated Fanny's reaction to her surroundings and further antagonized his wife with obstinate refusals to heed her plaintive cries.

Fanny's journal, a series of letters for her friend Elizabeth Sedgwick, reveals her growing sense of the horrors of slavery. Kemble at times transcribed the accounts of enslaved black women—letting their voices tell the story. Their tales are full of brutal sexual exploitation, skyrocketing infant mortality, multiple miscarriages. These beleaguered slave women sought relief and their pleas propelled Fanny on a disaster course. Her husband would brook no interference with plantation management, causing clash after clash between the couple during their months in the South.

These exhausting battles came to a head one night when a hysterical Kemble rowed a boat alone from Butler's Island to Darien to catch a steamer north. When she finally realized no steamer would be coming for days, Kemble returned to the plantation. A descendent speculated that Fanny's flight may have been prompted by the discovery of her husband's sexual liaison with a slave woman. In any case, we know that when the Butlers returned to Philadelphia in May 1839, they were estranged: Fanny was refusing her husband the marriage bed.

The couple continued to bicker and spent the next winter at odds. Butler went south without Fanny, despite her protests. Over the next few years, conditions steadily worsened between the couple. In November 1843, after accidentally coming across letters proving her husband's infidelities, Fanny requested a legal separation, retaining Theodore Sedgwick as counsel. In a fury, Butler reduced his wife's access to the children to one hour per day and for the next two years their relationship was governed by written contracts—including a specific clause prohibiting any communication with the Sedgwicks. Butler controlled the children, which allowed him to dictate ridiculous terms.

During this period of extreme marital alienation, Butler was accused of committing adultery with the wife of one of his close friends. Philadelphia was scandalized as Butler fought a duel with the injured husband—James Schott, who named Butler as correspondent in his highly publicized divorce. Fanny finally abandoned all hope of salvaging her relationship with her husband and was prepared to leave her children behind and set sail for London in October 1845. She reluctantly faced a separation from her daughters, but felt she had no alternative. Back in England, Kemble had to return to the stage to support herself.

Elizabeth Sedgwick had repeatedly intervened on Butler's behalf early in the marriage, but eventually became one of his severest critics. She called him a monster when he withheld letters to the girls from their mother abroad. (Sedgwick arranged for Kemble's letters to reach Sarah and Fan through friends in Philadelphia.) Two years later, Butler filed for divorce, charging Fanny with abandonment. When she heard the news, Kemble returned to the States in May 1848 to defend herself at great personal cost, forced to cancel lucrative bookings. Kemble had found acting roles too taxing. She could not withstand the strain of regular theatrical performances, but had been building a new career by offering Shakespearean readings.

Humiliated by Butler's grounds for divorce, Kemble wanted to be with her children, wanted to defend herself against his base claims. The Butler divorce became the object of speculation on both sides of the Atlantic, reported in the international press. The two young girls, aged thirteen and ten, became pawns in their parents' war.

But when do we get to the *real* war? Let me elliptically report that the divorce agreement, an out-of-court settlement in 1849, was not amicable. Butler was granted sole custody until his girls reached the age of eighteen. Although Fanny was promised a $1,500 annuity and two-months-a-year visitation, she complained she never received any alimony and Butler blocked her visits to the girls, intercepted her letters, and remained hostile for many years.[18] The girls were sent to boarding school and Kemble retreated to Europe.

Fanny and her older daughter, Sarah, were reunited after Sarah's eighteenth birthday in 1856. They celebrated by spending a summer together in the Berkshires, at Kemble's favorite haunt, in Lenox.

Simultaneously, Pierce Butler was plagued by severe financial setbacks; gambling and speculation forced him to put his business affairs in receivership.[19] By 1859, he had to endure the added humiliation of a public auction, selling off more than half his Georgia slaves. This auction caught not only the attention of sympathetic Southerners, but the northern press turned the spotlight on Butler's plight, trumpeting his shame in New York headlines. Butler tried to conduct himself with dignity during the sale, when he was forced to part with over three hundred "Butler people."

Broken in health and spirit, Pierce Butler retreated to Europe in 1859, when once again Fanny returned to America to spend time with both daughters after Fan turned eighteen. That same year, Sarah married Philadelphia doctor Owen Wister with her parents' approval, and Fanny took daughter Fan on a European tour.

Both Sarah and Fan had suffered during their parents' tumultuous marriage, lengthy separation, and messy divorce. The aftershocks of the couple's bitter estrangement continued throughout Butler and Kemble's lifetime.

Fan, at a more tender age when her mother left her father, bore the brunt of emotional trauma. Both girls had a blind loyalty to their father, as Sarah's only son, Owen, later recalled: "I was brought up to revere my grandfather. He did indeed make both his daughters adore him."[20] And both daughters found their mother extremely difficult, even as grown women. As Sarah confided: "My mother was the most stimulating companion I have ever known. She was also the most goading."[21]

Fanny was in Philadelphia on July 14, 1860, for the birth of

Sarah and Fanny Butler.
Courtesy of Coastal Georgia
Historical Society.

her first grandson, Sarah's only child, Owen Wister Jr. (called Dan to distinguish him from his father). Both parents and daughters all lived in Philadelphia on the very brink of the Civil War. The family and the national mood reflected restless discord rather than harmony.[22]

Despite loyalty to her father, and even though she found her mother trying, Sarah Wister was indelibly influenced by Kemble's political views and told Fanny in 1865: "I suppose the impressions you gave me as a child had never been effaced."[23] After Sarah married into the Wister family, she had pledged her allegiance to a liberal Yankee clan. This put a slight strain on her relationship with her sister, as Fan complained that Sarah went so far as to refuse to "receive a Southerner in her house."[24]

As secession fever heated up, both girls found themselves caught in a quagmire, along with many families of their generation. Yet the circumstances within the Butler-Kemble family were exceptional: the debate over slavery, which had figured so prominently in the Butler marital disagreements, was now leading to the breakdown of national harmony and perhaps even war. The Butler sisters remained civil to one another, although they maintained diametrically opposed political views on Confederate independence.

With South Carolina's Ordinance of Secession, a Pennsylvanian reported, "Butler is eager for secession & has just returned from Georgia, where he says there is no difference of opinion. He said that he came here [to Philadelphia] only to buy arms and intends to return immediately and join the army. He will take his daughter Fanny with him and has bought a rifle for *her,* too, for he says even the women of the South are going to fight."[25] Apparently this was false bravado, because six months later, Pierce Butler confided to his daughter Sarah that he would remain loyal to Pennsylvania and "would not take up arms against his own country even if Fanny [his daughter] & [Sarah] were not in existence as a restraining motive."[26] This could be Butler talking out of both sides of his mouth or shaping his sentiments depending upon which daughter he was addressing. Butler apparently transplanted the southern obsession with state loyalty to his birthplace of Pennsylvania and said he could not turn against his state. Despite this, Butler was a staunch advocate of Confederate independence.

By this time, Philadelphia had become a tinderbox. Following reports from Ft. Sumter in April 1861, Sarah Wister recorded that thousands assembled in the streets and swore "revenge on all disunionists." During the melee that followed, Sarah mentioned, "Oh how thankful I am for Father's absence."[27]

Pierce Butler had not gone alone to the South, indeed he had offered to accompany distant cousins south on his way to St. Simon's, providing Elizabeth Middleton Fisher, who went to visit her Charleston kin, an escort. Butler also took his daughter Fan on a plantation visit. Fan, by now, was a spirited rebel, even though she planned to return from Georgia to Philadelphia in April 1861. Sarah reported: "She thinks that the taking of Ft. Sumter will put an end to hostilities as the North will see that the South is in earnest, & is so very unwilling to fight itself!!! She will open her eyes a little when she arrives here and finds every man of her acquaintance enlisted." The display of flags and cockades greeted Fan when she returned to live with the Wisters. Sarah wrote, "I have no good qualities at all, small patriotism, no hero-worship & entire absence of curiosity."[28] But her diary tells another story, as she threw herself passionately into Union war work—preparing supplies for soldiers, sewing uniforms, soliciting charitable donations.

The sectional tensions during this period provoked a terrible emotional crisis for Sarah. Shortly after the news about Ft. Sumter, Sarah visited Butler Place: "A longing for home violets came over me, so instead of going to church . . . I picked quite a bunch & strayed back with them. It always seems strange to me to go to that place & now how much stranger than ever, that dear place; next to Owen, Father & Fan I love it above all things; I had the strongest yearning towards it to-day, before long it may be confiscated."[29]

Sarah pointedly does not include Kemble on this list. Mother and daughter were going through a particularly rough patch, with Fanny as her daughter's houseguest, excited about politics and overgenerous with advice about childrearing. To Sarah, she had long overstayed her welcome. On the eve of her departure, Owen suggested that Fanny prolong her visit. When Fanny offered to remain ensconced, Sarah declined her mother's offer to postpone her visit to New York and "went to bed more angry with Owen for his thoughtlessness & folly than I have been since our marriage."[30]

Sarah had just gotten some relief, her mother only gone a few days, when Fan returned, full of Confederate fire. When the sisters' birthday rolled around in late May, Sarah confessed to dreaming of Butler Place and scribbled in her journal: "Feeling that it might be the last of these double birthdays we might spend together I looked through all my jewelry to find something for her. . . . I have a choking ball in my throat."[31]

At times, Sarah could and did get very irritated with her sister, obsessed about all matters military and offering running commentary.[32] In July when Fanny repeated false war rumors, Sarah groaned with annoyance: "Like mother like daughter, a wonderful pair, not a word of it true."[33]

Both daughters were distinctly relieved when their father reappeared, safe and sound, in Philadelphia on August 3, 1861, after nearly five months in the South. It was a great shock when Butler was arrested on August 18, by special order of Secretary of War Cameron, and taken to New York for incarceration.

Sarah confided her fears for her unmarried sister: "Poor little thing, this will come more heavily on her than on anyone else after her winter & spring of anxiety and harassment." She also confessed suspicions that Butler might be guilty of aiding and abetting the Confederacy.[34] Fanny Kemble wrote a friend: "The charges against him is that he acted as an agent for the Southerners in a visit he paid this spring, having received large sums of money for the purchase and transmission of arms. Knowing Mr. B[utler']s Southern sympathies, I think the charge very likely to be true; whether it can be proved is quite another question."[35]

Mother and daughters were surprisingly united on this issue. Despite their divided political agendas and despite Kemble's marital estrangement, Fanny, Sarah, and Fan were all three united by a campaign to obtain Butler's release. They were convinced that the government had no case and hoped no evidence could be dredged up to convict him.

The Wisters turned to their great friends, the Fox family and the Fishers who lived nearby in Branchtown and had strong political connections in Washington, to intercede on Butler's behalf. On August 22, Sarah sent a personal note to the White House, directly to President Lincoln. She asked permission to communicate with her father, who was reportedly being held incommunicado. On August 23, Sarah received a note from Butler, sketching the ordeal of his confinement at Ft. Lafayette on Staten Island where he was denied any visitors. She was devastated by his report of conditions: "Whatever right the government may have to arrest & imprison men on suspicion, it cannot have the least to herd them together . . . & deprive them of all necessaries and decencies of life."[36] Despite their bleak mood, Sarah and Fanny made a planned trip to Lenox to be with their mother on August 26. Owen wrote his wife good news on August 30: a search of her father's papers by federal authorities had turned up no incriminating evidence. The next day he reported to Sarah: "I received today thro Fox a permission from Genl. Scott for you and Fan to pay your father a visit."[37]

Butler was released by order of the State Department on September 21. Although he was welcomed home with open arms by both daughters, an Autumn chill was in the air. Sidney George Fisher complained: "He [Butler] refused to take the Oath of Allegiance and is morally as much a traitor as any man in the Confederate army."[38]

Both Butler and his daughter Fan were forced to muzzle their unpopular secessionist views. In 1862 Fanny returned to Europe and brought Fan with her to tour Switzerland. When Kemble visited London, she was alarmed by the political friction between England and the United States, the sense of divided British loyalties. She feared the British might offer diplomatic recognition to the Confederacy. At this dramatic juncture, Fanny Kemble consented to publish her *Journal of Residence on a Georgian Plantation,* her record of her time on the Butler plantation in the winter of 1838–39.

When Lydia Maria Child had suggested that Kemble publish her eyewitness account of slavery in 1841, Pierce Butler and Fanny clashed violently over the issue, as they had so many other times over Fanny's writings, and over her views on slavery. While they were still married, Butler prevailed, and publication of this abolitionist journal was suppressed. But during the war, Kemble felt publishing her journal could sway British public opinion against slavery, and, divorced for over a decade, she thought it was important to assert her right to publish her own writing despite any embarrassment it might cause Butler. She also included for publication an unpublished letter condemning slavery, which was composed for the *London Times* in 1852 following the controversy over Harriet Beecher Stowe's *Uncle Tom's Cabin.* So in a sense Kemble was venting decades of abolitionist ire. Her eyewitness account and her impassioned letter were formidable propaganda.

When Kemble's Georgia journal appeared in England in May 1863, it met with favorable reviews. A critic writing in the *Athenaeum* pronounced, "A more startling and fearful narrative on a well-worn subject was never laid before readers."[39] Parts of it were read on the floor of the House of Commons, and excerpts were read aloud to cotton workers in Manchester to stir up antislavery fervor. An American edition appeared a few months later.

Fanny's daughters had differing opinions about this publication. Sarah herself was a poet, translator, essayist, and, as a Union sympathizer, saw the value of her mother's literary contribution. Sarah was involved in abolitionist circles where authors were frequently asked to contribute work to raise money and stir up sympathy for the antislavery cause, as Maria Weston Chapman's *Liberty Bell* had done for years. This was an effective ploy to involve literary celebrities and to bring respectability and a wider following to antislavery activism. Sarah perhaps viewed her mother's journal as part of this abolitionist literary tradition of which she approved and to which she subscribed.

Fan, however, viewed this book not merely as a scandalous piece of political propaganda but as a symbol of family betrayal. She railed at her mother's continuing disregard for Pierce Butler's feelings—and Fanny's insensitivity to her own daughter's feelings as well. Nevertheless, in the Spring of 1864, Fan went abroad to stay with her mother in an English cottage, and the two planned to tour Italy the next year. Perhaps this was an elaborate bribery scheme on Fanny's part to soothe her daughter's ruffled feathers. Despite their differences, the two women were willing to spend time together—trying to keep open the lines of communication and recapture lost years.

When news of the fall of Richmond, the end of the war, finally came, Kemble confided she and her daughter both wept over the news: "I with joy and she with sorrow."[40] But surrender interrupted plans for a Continental tour as Fan returned home to her father, who needed both his daughters at this critical juncture. His estates were in complete disarray and the years of disruption had taken a ruinous toll.

Butler was offered twenty thousand dollars a year to lease half of his sea island plantations immediately after the war. This would have afforded income and leisure, which he sorely could have used after the rough financial blow of his slave auction just before the war. Yet Butler refused. When he heard that many of "his people," former slaves, had returned to Butler Island and other holdings, he was pleased. When he discovered that even some of the people who had been sold away in 1859 were now back on the island seeking a home, Butler was gratified. He foolishly determined to return to the business of planting, something that he had left to others for most of his career as a landowner. Nevertheless, he headed South with high hopes—to manage his war-torn estates himself, to throw himself into the fray as he had never before. Fan Butler, like her mother before her, was determined to accompany Pierce Butler despite his objections. She was convinced that together they might achieve his ambitious goal. In March 1866, Fan and her father left Philadelphia "to look after [their] property in Georgia and see what could be done about it."[41]

The Butler farmstead, plundered during Yankee occupation, was in worse shape than they had imagined. Butler became exhausted, drained by the challenge of management. His daughter tried to lessen his burdens, but she, too, was sapped by worries and drudgery. Both were delighted when Sarah brought her son to pay an extended visit: "It is a great pleasure to Fanny to have us here. . . . He [Pierce Butler] said yesterday morning that it made him so happy it seemed like a dream."[42]

Sarah expressed her concerns in a letter home to her husband: "Fan has a hard time. The blacks give her as much trouble as the Irish do, tho they are not impertinent. . . . She has the most minute directions to give about everything & to see that they are carried out, besides. I helped her plant a row of tomatoes on Saturday and she has put in with her own hands or superintended the putting in of all the vegetables that have been planted this spring. She looks much better than when she left home, but is pale & rather thin & I think dejected by the uncertainty of her future."[43]

"Dejected by uncertainty" captured the entire South's mood. Other planter refugees who returned home to estates after surrender faced not only a rebellious labor force but also the specter of Union occupation. The financial hardships of Reconstruction were oppressive for those whites used to luxurious circumstances. The autonomy of the black labor force created new wrinkles. Butler tried to re-impose previous patterns of fieldwork, which were unacceptable to free labor. The entire enterprise seemed more than the father-daughter duo could manage.

In June 1866 Fanny and her father attended the funeral of a revered St. Simon's figure, James Hamilton Couper, an internationally known botanist and master planter who saw his lands and his family destroyed by war. The funeral was a dismal affair, at a church vandalized by Yankees at Frederica. Fan complained, "Someday justice will be done, and the Truth shall be heard above the political din of slander and lies, and the Northern people shall see things as they are, and not through the dark veil of envy, hatred and malice."[44] Fan was being consumed by her anger during her months in Georgia.

In the summer of 1867, Butler put his foot down and insisted that his daughter return North to stay with her sister. When she left her father behind, it was with great trepidation. And, most unfortunate for the sensitive Fan, Butler succumbed to malaria in August, which hit both daughters very hard. Sarah Wister seemed overwhelmed by grief. To make matters worse, her mother had moved into the Wisters' home within weeks of Butler's death. Fanny was traveling with an English maid and the duo were an unwelcome addition to Sarah's household. She confided to Fan, "I wd gladly pass the winter in Siberia if I cd have some solitude there."[45]

Fan managed to control her grief and threw herself into tackling the project her father started. She returned to the Georgia plantations she and her sister inherited, with brother-in-law Owen Wister in tow. Sarah wrote sardonically to her husband in November 1867: "I am sorry that Fanny is destined to encounter opposition & disappointment in her plans, whatever they are, but it could hardly be otherwise."[46]

Certainly Fan Butler was up against formidable obstacles. Tunis G. Campbell, an African American activist, preached black equality and fueled discontent among freedpeople cropping Butler land. Fan Butler took a tough line with those who worked for her: "One or two, who seemed rather more inclined to be insolent than the rest, I dismissed, always saying, 'You are free to leave the place, but not to stay here and behave as you please, for I am free too, and moreover own the place, and so have a right to give my orders on it, and have them obeyed.'"[47] After Owen returned North, Fan Butler remained devoted to her vigil, to resurrect the plantations, to carry on her father's work on estates for which he gave up his very name, the place where he had perished pursuing his dreams.

Fan Butler deserted her post only for brief intervals, visits North and to England where she became acquainted with the relatives of her suitor, the Reverend James Leigh. She had met him in the North and invited him down to visit her Georgian estates. They eventually decided to marry.

They were wed in a ceremony in England in June 1871. Fanny Kemble was happy with her daughter's choice of this gentle, easygoing cleric, even though she was clearly disappointed that her daughter continued her crusade in the sea islands. Fanny Kemble had little patience with the idea of restoring the Butler holdings to prewar glory, as she had both experienced and condemned life on the plantations. Nevertheless, Fanny Butler Leigh and her new husband decided to return to Georgia to cultivate rice and oranges.

The news from St. Simon's was full of disappointment as a fire had done extensive damage to the rice mill and several buildings. Also Fanny Leigh reported: "The teacher I had left on the Island to train and educate the people, not only intellectually but morally, had turned out very badly, and had led one of my nicest young servant girls astray, which, with the other disaster, so disheartened me."[48] But James Leigh prevailed, and new seed was bought, English laborers were imported, and repairs were undertaken to settle in and fulfill their mission.

Severe financial setbacks, trouble with labor, ill health, low spirits all plagued the Leighs during their tenure in Georgia. It was a doomed experiment not only because Fanny Leigh was really trying to rebuild the Butler estates into a splendor she had never enjoyed but also because a principled Anglican clergyman and his bride were little prepared to shoulder the burdens required to turn the operation to a profit.

The Leighs moved between family homes in Philadelphia,

where their daughter Alice was born in 1874, and their plantations in Georgia. They spent summers in the North, mindful that Pierce Butler succumbed to illness during August. Sarah Wister came to visit her sister for a month in the winter, but the downward spiral continued. When the Leighs lost their second child, a boy born in January 1877, a son they named Pierce Butler Leigh who died after only twenty-four hours, Fan's spirits were shattered. She was finally willing to give up her Georgia venture and go back to England with her husband. The Leighs made arrangement for their rice crop before sailing for England where the Reverend, well connected and amiable, was able to secure a comfortable parish.

While her sister had undertaken ambitious schemes to reconstruct their Georgia plantations, Sarah Wister endured her own difficulties. She reflected on her wartime experience: "The strain of the war was such as nobody who did not live then can fancy; household matters were difficult, our mode of life monotonous yet irregular, & very hard to manage; my duties at the Sanitary Rooms continued; I kept up my social relations by a dreary semi-annual round of visits, two or three hundred, generally on foot; of social pleasures outside my own house I had nearly none; I taught my child & had him a great deal with me."[49] Sarah and Owen both complained of severe physical ailments during this period. Owen was forced to undertake several rest cures after a collapse due to overwork during the war.

The onset of Sarah's deep depression—which she later explained was a nervous collapse followed by two years of melancholia—propelled the couple out of their Philadelphia environs. The Wisters set sail for Europe in 1870, where they wandered from London to France to Italy, touring with Fanny Kemble and becoming great friends with Henry James.

And when Fanny Butler Leigh moved to England with her husband and child, the family had an opportunity to be reunited—to mesh together into a harmonious blend. One would hope that time might salve the wounds. Perhaps the death of Pierce Butler could have muffled family discord.

But when Fanny Butler Leigh gave birth to a second son in 1879, and insisted upon naming the boy after her father, volcanic eruptions reigned. Fanny Kemble apparently had her heart set on her daughter naming the child William Shakespeare Leigh, especially as his father was now a vicar in a very fashionable parish in Stratford. But when her mother *refused* to attend the christening because Fan persisted and named the baby Pierce Butler Leigh, young Fanny was enraged. This precipitated a permanent coolness, near estrangement between mother and daughter. When her second male child died a little over a year old, Fan became unhinged.

Family correspondence indicates there were other matters at play. When Sarah expressed her concerns to her sister, she acknowledged Fan's problems; many dated back further than her grief over losing her child: "For over a year I have thought yr letters hardly those of a person in their right mind; even before the little boy's birth, before your pregnancy. The total confusion of dates, figures, facts, the complete preoccupation with yr. self the groundless sense of universal grievance were like the productions of a mind off its balance. . . . Now if any such terrible consequence shd overtake you there will be nobody to blame but yr. self. . . . If I have been so unfortunate as to wound or offend you in this letter it is most unintentional. It is written with the most sincere affection, pity, & solicitude."[50] Sarah had inherited her mother's penchant for bluntness.[51] But she had gone through her own bouts of mental illness and was issuing a strict warning to her sister that she was losing ground.

Fan Leigh's fury with her mother fueled bouts of hysteria during this period. After Fan had subjected her mother to an ugly tirade concerning Pierce Butler while the two were in Paris during one of their tours, Fanny confided she was unable to talk freely to her younger daughter ever since, as sadly "our intercourse is one of the tragic consequences of life."[52]

Fan lashed out at Kemble, as her mother was preparing the second installment of her memoirs, *Records of Later Life.* The first installment began as a series of articles in the *Atlantic Monthly.* The series's popularity fueled an annotated and expanded version, the three volume *Records of Girlhood.* Kemble's planned continuation would narrate the story of her life, culled from diary entries and letters, past her American tour and marriage, covering the period of her divorce. Fan sent her mother a stinging request in a letter dated May 1, 1881:

> My dearest Mother
> You have said over & over again that you thought people most unjustified in writing personal reminiscences of others which would be painful to their relations and friends. Then how come you think of writing about a person no longer alive whose memory is sacred & honored by his children & whom what you wrote would give the greatest pain and those children yours too! Does being their mother give you the right to wound and distress them? You have also said several times that you would not publish your memoirs after your marriage. . . . Why have you changed your mind about our right to express an opinion as to whether or not we should like it published. . . . I have never

lost in the least degree by the feeling of bitterness I have always felt about the publication of your first Southern book [*Journal of Residence on a Georgian Plantation*] wh. nothing would ever induce me to have it in the house. . . . I never can forgive it. . . . Any mention you make of him or your life in America which treats the time you were living with him as his wife must be intensely painful to me. I implore you not to alienate my affection from you entirely by doing it.

Your loving daughter

F.

Kemble responded tersely: "My dear Fanny, I can only acknowledge your letter, I cannot answer it otherwise than by saying that I must myself be the judge of what I think to write and publish and of course accept the consequences of doing so."[53] One wonders here what other kinds of intimate exchanges this follows, as such a brief response from Kemble is rare.

Fan tried to enlist her sister's support in her campaign to censor their mother, complaining: "If she repeats her Southern experiences or in any way alludes to her married relations I do not think I can ever see or speak to her again." She wrote disparagingly about her mother's achievements with *Records of Girlhood* (1879): "The success of her first book has so aroused her vanity and love of notoriety that the desire to keep herself before the public is irresistible."[54]

Over her younger daughter's vehement objections, Fanny Kemble published *Records of Later Life* in 1882. Kemble removed as many personal references as she could, masking identities and other measures, a consideration her daughter Fan failed to appreciate. Indeed, Fanny Butler Leigh launched a counteroffensive by preparing her own book, a kind of counterpoint recollections: *Ten Years on a Georgian Plantation since the War,* published in 1883. Leigh wanted to offer an alternate vision of life in the sea islands, one intended to correct the distortions created by Kemble's journal. Fan's Georgian journal was a figurative retort, a slap at her mother's testimony. Particularly in the "Addenda" Fanny the younger takes aim at Fanny senior: "The question whether slavery is or is not a moral wrong I do not wish or intend to discuss. . . . I doubt our slaves being willing to change places with the free English labourer of those days [the 1820s], had the change been offered him. . . . They [slaves] did not suffer under the system [slavery] or regard it with the horror they were supposed to do by all the advocates of abolition."[55] Throughout her discussion of the challenge of free labor and the easier time African Americans once had being taken care of by their masters (rather than having to struggle to earn their own keep as free labor), Leigh offers pointed and repeated claims of racial superiority. She closes her book with the notion that emancipation freed the owners from the "terrible load of responsibility which slavery entailed."

Fanny Leigh's entire book, but especially those final chapters, were meant to overturn the view of slavery popularized by her mother. The younger Fanny hoped her own eyewitness account of life on her St. Simon's plantations, with excerpts from antebellum letters and other supporting material, might undermine her mother's autobiographical writings. Fanny took deadly aim and blasted away.

In spite of these violent clashes, family ties prevailed. The sisters had rough periods, but generally patched up their differences. Perhaps they had formed an unbreakable bond, clinging to one another as their parents' marriage crumbled and they were shipped off to school together. The bonds of sisterhood withstood the test of time. Sarah was frequently irritated by her sister, but rarely wounded. And Fan appeared more annoyed, rather than hurt, by their episodic scrapes.

Even mother and daughters were able to re-establish civil, although not particularly warm, relations, until the end of Kemble's life. When Fanny Kemble became completely infirm and housebound, her daughter Fan took her in. Sarah commented sympathetically on her mother in 1889 when she came to England to visit, "I found a change for wh. her letters had not in the least prepared me. I found a childish old woman . . . no longer a rational being. Yet I pity her so much that I feel it easier to get on with her than ever before."[56] Fanny Kemble died in the Leigh home in England in 1893.

The Butler daughters clung to their Georgia patrimony, with amicable partitions of their holdings in 1894. Attempts to sell their sea island estates followed, as the close of the century approached; it seemed time to sever ties even though no sale was concluded, no suitable buyer found until 1908, the very same year Sarah Wister died (in the same house in which she had been born, Butler Place). Her younger sister, Fanny Leigh, who had married into the British gentry and presented her daughter at court, died at her home in England in 1910.

Like many other families, the Butler daughters wanted to put the Civil War—and its conflicted meanings—behind them. Even while in exile abroad, they seemed haunted by the divide. They had the luxury to escape the places that reminded them of loss, unlike thousands of families with less means. But no one could escape the memories.

The indelibility of the war's impact on the postwar American aristocracy remains a topic ripe for renewed scholarly research. Until recently such analysis might be tarred as "apologist." But now a very sophisticated and provocative "memory industry" seems to be going into high gear. New work on memory and memorials of the Civil War from David Blight, Earl Mulderink, LeeAnn Whites, Thomas Brown, and Anastatia Sims, among others, promises to give us fresh and important perspectives.

One of the most distinctive tales of war's impact was penned by Edith Wharton over a hundred years ago. "The Lamp of Psyche" was published in *Scribner's* in 1895, one of Wharton's very first short stories to appear in print.[57] The tale provides an understated, acid portrait of those men who "sat out the war" and the circumstances surrounding women's role in keeping sacrifice and its meaning alive—for northern women. Wharton's own father did not see military service, but the young Edith was voracious in her appetite for stories of wartime heroics. She read widely about this great dramatic era that transformed her country. Perhaps this story, one of her earliest pieces of fiction, was semiautobiographical. It may have touched a nerve within Wharton's family, and even though her *Scribner's* editor, Edward Burlingame, implored, Wharton refused to allow the piece to be included in her collection of short stories, *The Greater Inclination* (1899).

As the story opens Delia Corbett is a blissful wife. She had been widowed "past thirty" and expected to live her life diminished and alone, but was rescued, "given the one portion denied to all other women on earth, the immense, the unapproachable privilege of becoming Laurence Corbett's wife." The fictional Corbetts are from the eastern seaboard elite, but like the Wisters, they join a class of drifters during their nomadic travels in Europe. An illness of Delia Corbett's aunt back home in Boston causes disturbances in the field. Although her husband is not particularly interested in returning to his birthplace and ancestral home, Delia, also from Boston, is drawn back. She not only wants to see her beloved and ailing aunt but also to essentially show-off her remarriage. She was an unhappy wife the first time around, and her pleasure with her new life is such that she wants to shine in former circles.

During her sojourn in Boston, Delia's Aunt Mary casually inquires about Corbett when she has Delia alone: "Then, of course he was in the war. . . . You've never told me about that. Did he see active service?" This question hits Delia like an unexpected tremor, a tingle that hints at disaster.

Delia begins to think about that which she has apparently and self-protectively repressed: "All the men of her family, all the men of her friends' families, had fought in the war; Mrs. Hayne's [Aunt Mary's] husband had been killed at Bull Run, and one of Delia's cousins at Gettysburg. Ever since she could remember it had been regarded as a matter of course by those about her that every man of her husband's generation who was neither lame, halt, nor blind should have fought in the war." Delia tries to smother her emotions and coolly responds: "I really don't know. I never asked him."

Wharton offers her character an intriguing dissemblance. How can a girl raised within a society that measures a man and his good name by whether or not he chalked up Union military service, how can she have not been curious about her husband's role in the Civil War? Perhaps because they both were set adrift in Europe—a place purposely disassociated with the war, the subject could be avoided. Again, this was the place where Sarah Wister, emerging from her years of deep depression, and her husband Owen, following his breakdown due to wartime service, fled for several years.

They were joined by hundreds of others, from the North

but especially the South—from the former first lady, Varina Davis, to the Langhorne belles of Virginia (one of whom became Lady Astor). During the quarter century following the Civil War, the American aristocracy sailed in droves across the Atlantic, absorbed by the Grand Tour and on a great escape. But can crossing an ocean allow you to forget?

In Wharton's tale, it is the return to America and the voice of a war widow, whose polite but firm dose of reality bursts her niece's bubble, that initiates Delia's torment, forcing her to confront what she has malignantly neglected. The slow dawning of truth is Wharton at her best. The couple returns to Paris with Delia's "increasing fear of her aunt's unspoken verdict."

Delia's dread envelopes her, slowly sealing her off from her happiness and her husband. The once-contented wife becomes an island of apprehension, until Corbett, fatefully, provides an opening for her to pop the question. And hope against hope is crushed, just like the crystal on a miniature portrait of a Union soldier Corbett purchases for his wife in a shop on the Rue Bonaparte. Inscribed on the back, "Fell at Chancellorsville, May 3, 1863," his little gift for her, a remembrance of their shared past, allows Delia to ask him what she has long wondered: what did Corbett do during the war, what was it that prevented him from enlisting?

Corbett's vague and diffident response shatters Delia's world. Corbett was indeed one of the despised set: those without a sense of honor, who put self-interest and self-preservation above patriotism when their country needed them most. Love is instantly transformed and the light of Delia's life is extinguished by this terrible truth. The giddy quality of Delia Corbett's elation over her marriage in Wharton's opening is matched in intensity by the gloom that overtakes her heroine by the story's closing paragraphs, as she realizes she is forever chained to this man she can no longer respect or admire.

Wharton's story illuminates another important postwar truth. Wharton highlights the legend Americans hoped to perpetuate—that although each side was *passionately* devoted to its cause, both sides were united in the righteousness of their independent pursuit of honor. Once war ended, they could claim common and honorable ground. The Union stalwarts and Confederate guardians of the flame become bosom buddies, promoting propaganda that captured imaginations both North and South. This theatrical concoction held the country together as veterans slowly began to commingle reunions. Triumph and loss were blended into a legend of shared military valor.

Certainly the South has been characterized as a region soaked in memory, a region so rich with the past it remains drenched with nostalgia, dripping with retrospection. The Union created its own cult of glory, as Grand Army of the Republic posts dotted towns from the rocky shores of Maine to the midwestern plains. The Yankees planted tons of marble on town squares as statues of veterans embellished and admonished. The literal enshrinement of the village of Gettysburg embodies this movement. The town embraced its epic role and became a symbol of Union commemoration.

In the battles over memorials and glory, the daughters of Fanny Kemble struggled passionately to maintain equilibrium, to balance the competing and conflicting elements that had pulled them apart during wartime. Even the next generation, represented by Owen Wister, found itself caught up in this extraordinary problem of regional and national identity.[58]

Those families who survived the American Civil War did

not remain unscathed. Evidence indicates their children, and their children's children, found peace alone could not heal all the wounds.

Because of the extraordinary circumstances that befell Fanny Kemble and her girls, their stories force us to ponder the complex legacy of our Civil War. We can recognize that a sister divided against her sister is just as powerful an image as the constant recasting of the battle as a "brother's war." And finally, battles between mothers and daughters are perhaps even more tempestuous and challenging for us to chart than those between fathers and sons.

CHAPTER TWO

Orphans of the Storm

Steering a New Course

I WAS COMPELLED TO EXPLORE THE SUBJECT OF Civil War orphans for a number of reasons. My main interest at the present time is to generate enthusiasm so others will march off and do more research on this neglected topic. So my rather random tales of woe and very slight bits and pieces of wisdom are mere fragments that I hope will some day fit into a larger mosaic of the impact of the Civil War on children.[1]

I stumbled onto one of the areas of Civil War studies that is literally crying out for research. It has been right there under our noses and somehow we have ignored it. I cannot imagine who could continue to ignore a wailing, abandoned child—the orphans of the storm, a storm that swept across our nation, touching everything in its indelible wake.

For me it was twin disasters that focused my attention on the subject of orphans. First, a very noisy Georgian, the Speaker of the House of Representatives, brought the whole topic of orphanages screaming into the headlines in 1995. During this same period, one of my friends sardonically welcomed me to the "Orphans Club," as my widowed mother had recently died, and there I was: an orphan. I became almost fixated on this word, and its resonance drew me into the stacks and archives. As a historian, I was astonished at what I did not find. As a Civil War historian, I was appalled.

Most of us know without having to be reminded that the Civil War was a colossal bloodbath, a slaughter. An entire generation of young men was wiped out: roughly 630,000 died, with over half a million wounded. And those that weren't maimed were scarred, regardless.

Some of you may well remember that on a *single day* at Antietam nearly 4,800 Americans were killed—when only four thousand were killed during the *entire* Revolutionary War. We hear these boggling numbers, but we need to think about this on a more human scale. In the small Massachusetts town of Worcester, over four thousand of its adult male population of twenty-four thousand went marching off to war—one out of six—and of those nearly *five hundred* never came back—one out of eight soldiers perished. When we try to imagine this in present day terms, it is a loss of astronomical proportions. Think of the agony families suffered with losses in the recent Gulf War, and even more dramatically, with the Vietnam War. These losses combined were but a drop in the bucket of blood shed by Americans in the nineteenth century during one year of the Civil War.

And while the northern population grew with the influx of European immigrants (many who themselves fought in Irish companies and German brigades), the white South dwindled. Many black Southerners fled to fight with the Union Army. The population in the South was considerably depleted from war deaths. The minority who went into exile following the war were a loss that could barely be sustained after such crushing battle tolls. For so many Americans, the Civil War meant a loss of sons and brothers. Perhaps because of the youth of both armies we have too long dwelt on this particular aspect—the sadness of sweethearts perishing, marriages unmade and children unborn. But the war also very dramatically meant a loss of husbands and particularly *fathers,* which resulted in orphans by the thousands, a literal gusher of fatherless children following each successive battle.

The American Civil War was the single most devastating factor in terms of nineteenth-century parental loss. More children became orphans than at any other time during the century, and the government's inadequate resources meant the problem was dealt with poorly during the war and little better after. You might imagine such a tremendous and catastrophic loss generated a mass social response—and on that score you may be right. But if you think this widespread response is chronicled, even thinly, in secondary literature, you would be entirely wrong.

The library shelves are stacked high with books on juvenile delinquency and runaways. Crime and deviance have attracted consistent and quality attention from sociologists, psychologists, and even historians. Foster care in modern America does have a respectable literature, but what came before World War II remains a relatively unexplored mystery. European historians have done pioneering and fascinating research on abandoned children, on orphans and social responses to both. But to seek informative texts on American orphans is a losing proposition.

Scouring catalogs at the Library of Congress and Widener Library at Harvard University, the two largest depositories available in the United States, you will be lucky to find a handful of items on orphans in America in the nineteenth century. I was only able to locate a handful of uninspiring monographs, mainly institutional studies (an exception being one recent work on a nineteenth century orphan asylum in New York state), but there are more sophisticated treatments of the orphan in literature and the architecture of orphanages than there are serious historical studies of the actual experiences of orphans.[2] Not one, but two major Broadway musicals (*Oliver!* and *Annie*) have been inspired by orphans, as scholarly trends continue to lag behind popular cultural embrace.

As is often the case, fiction writers have gotten ahold of a riveting subject and dealt with it powerfully—well ahead of scholars. Recall the historical truths evident in a prize-winning book such as *Beloved.* Toni Morrison in some way jump-started new views on the psychological and brutalizing aspects of American slavery.

Joan Brady published a very disturbing novel, *Theory of War,* which dealt with one of her ancestors who she felt was sold into slavery after the Civil War—by his own father, orphaned in the cruelest possible way.[3] The portrait of a sturdy white child stares out mournfully from the book's jacket. Her novel opens with the heart-wrenching tale of a white Civil War veteran losing his wife and "selling" his young son to a Kansas farmer as an apprentice, a farmworker—the boy will be indentured until he is grown.

The author's claim she descended from a "slave" interfered with what I thought could have been a valuable debate on the harshness of war and its aftermath. I was asked by the *Washington Post* to discuss the phenomenon of "white slaves" in a review of the book, a request that caused problems on several levels. Although I very much liked the novel and would recommend it highly, Brady overstates a case that does not have to be made in order for her book to be the searing indictment and gripping fable it remains.

The notion of whites held as slaves appears a sensational proposition. Some whites, it seems, were reduced to slave status in the seventeenth and eighteenth century; for example, a white woman in British colonial America lost her freedom if she married a slave, and she and her children were certainly treated as chattel. But the practice was not sustained, and white peonage could not be characterized as slavery in the nineteenth century. This exaggeration does a disservice, even if it is only jacket-copy hype.

We know hundreds, perhaps thousands of children were disposed of in this callous manner. It is somehow more compelling to have a powerful novelist tackle the subject. We can read several fictional and historical works detailing boxcar loads of kids shipped westward on "orphan trains." It was equally common that, for a price, hundreds of young children were turned over to virtual strangers as farm laborers during this era. Records of the Freedman's Bureau overflow with accounts chronicling abuse within the "apprentice system," a system that was all too similar to the banished system of slavery. But the placing of homeless children onto those farms where extra hands were welcome was the business of many orphanages in rural areas.

Annie Oakley's autobiographical writings detail her harrowing Ohio childhood. Born during the Civil War, Oakley was farmed out by her mother to the local children's home after her father's death propelled the family further along poverty's downward spiral. The tale becomes more bleak when, after a brief and fairly agreeable stay at the county home, Oakley is sent to live with a particularly cruel couple whom she refuses to name but refers to as the "Wolves."

At the age of eight, young Annie is forced to perform arduous labor from sunup to sundown, dressed in rags, denied proper food, turned out in the snow to die one night when her mistress has a fit of temper. Sick of the squalor, fed up with the relentless campaign to break her, young Annie ran away from her tormentors, shouldered a gun, and became a crack shot. She joined the Wild West Show and became the highest paid woman in nineteenth-century America—a rags to riches tale. Annie Oakley escaped Darke County and its grim memories of her orphan days.

But, Annie wasn't an orphan if her mother was still living, or was she? This is another topic that could use extensive investigation. To the best of my abilities, I have discerned that the use of the term *orphan* is not strictly applied in the nineteenth century to a child who has lost both parents. Rather, an orphan is any child who has lost a father, not to be confused with a natural or illegitimate child—a bastard, born "without" a proper father. Again, this whole question seems ripe for more exploration by social historians. However, the field seems to have been left to legal historians, who have done remarkable tracking and hunting. The fine monographs that have resulted raise interesting questions for those of us concerned with more than statutory evidence.

No child is born without a mother, but those who lose the maternal parent are referred to, quite sensibly, as "motherless." And in much of what I have read, a child without both mother and father is pointedly called "homeless" or more often a "homeless orphan." It was expected that homeless children would be taken in by a relative, and this relative was often designated long before parental death, as proper parents would determine a child's guardian designate. (Young William T. Sherman suffered the loss of his parents but was taken in by friends, as was common.) This practice seems not merely a function of class but a practical part of nineteenth-century family life, which parents of all stations observed. Many parents took care of the issue with "godparents." And this role seemed to embrace much more in the past than it does with us today.

If, however, no relative stepped forward on behalf of the "homeless child," then a close friend of the family might assume the duties. This explains why so many institutions used the term "Homes for the Friendless Orphan," to indicate those children bereft of the proper safety net.

Again, most of this is my intuition, extracted from documents replete with coded language. The guardians of these institutions understood the distinctions, as they wrote with passion and verve, but only rarely with any expository clarity. Someone, somewhere has surely prepared a key to help us understand these layers of meaning, these complex ramifications. For now I feel desperate for a locksmith—or perhaps younger, nimbler minds than mine—to crack the vault.

Certainly, we know most orphans who were not taken in by family and friends were cosseted by the church. With the rise of public institutions in the nineteenth century, several of these religious organizations secularized—seeking state funding and a wider mandate from the public for their good works. Some institutional histories reveal such evolutions.[4]

Antebellum Americans were hypersensitive to attempts on the part of religious communities to take in orphans. Each child was expected to be folded into its religious community, so that children would be raised by persons of the same faith as their parents. Within an increasingly transient and complex society, this did not always work. Frequently the city found itself saddled with a surplus of orphans. The Shakers seemed to have a relatively easy time integrating orphans into their rural settlements. They would volunteer to care for these homeless, friendless orphans within their celibate communities then offer each one, when he or she reached adulthood, the choice of remaining within the group or being given a token sum and sent out into the world. Many more males ventured out into the world at the age of eighteen than did female orphans, but the community kept its faith and its word. Several hundred antebellum orphans were given foster care by Shakers in this manner.

By contrast, Catholic orphanages, on the rise and expanding in American cities, were viewed with great suspicion. Any attempts on the part of Catholic institutions to take in children from non-Catholic families caused quite a stir. Protestant ministers might play upon these fears to rouse their own congregations to support orphanages so the Catholics might not "steal" children away from their Protestant faiths.

Increasingly churches saw orphanages as part of their mission within antebellum America, not just in urban centers, but throughout the countryside. The Kentucky Female Orphan School of Midway, Kentucky, was chartered in 1846 as a corporation by religious leaders. The three-fold purpose of this charitable endeavor: to clothe, feed, and educate orphan girls. When Robert Broadburst headed the school in the fall of 1858, he was guardian to twenty-four girls. He embarked on a program of expansion and by 1860 nearly doubled his enrollment to forty-five. By the end of the war, the dormitories were expanded to sleep 55. However by October 1865 seventy-five girls were living in housing intended to accommodate fifty. By the end of the school year in 1871 the school enrolled ninety-six young women. A committee was appointed to secure funds to endow the school. At this time not all the pupils were "dependents," as there were "pay pupils" as well. To reduce the distinction between those girls with means and those reduced to a "friendless" state, all the girls were required to share housework chores.

The schedule was rigorous. During the school year girls were expected to rise at five and breakfast at six. At other times, girls slept until 6 A.M. In the spring and early autumn school began at 8 A.M., with recess from 11:30 to 1:30 for the noontime meal and chores. Classes resumed from 1:30 to 5 P.M.—breaking earlier, at 4 P.M., during winter. After supper, all pupils observed a study period from 7 to 9 P.M. before an early bedtime.[5] Despite the strictness of the daily regimen, school officials adopted a lenient policy concerning discipline:

"No corporal punishment shall be inflicted under any circumstances nor shall mode of discipline calculated to degrade the pupil be adopted."[6] Kentucky, like so many southern states, juggled the increasing responsibilities the Civil War imposed.

One particularly poignant statistic: In 1866, 20 percent of the Mississippi state revenue was spent on artificial limbs. Friendless orphans were competing with limited sources. A monthly paper in Mississippi, the *Orphan's Home Banner*, encouraged generous giving: "For seven years the Orphans' Home of Mississippi has been sustained by the people; will you be willing to sustain it seven years longer . . . or will you allow the tears, prayers, labors, and money spent all be for naught?"[7]

South Carolina mounted several noble campaigns during the postwar era to support homes for the state's hundreds of orphans. Charleston had maintained an exemplary orphanage since the eighteenth century, and the city took great pride in its charitable institutions. But the bombardments of war, the scar of ruins blighting the city, took the wind out of the sails of charity within Charleston. One alarmed aristocrat reported in September 1865:

> Last evening about 8 o'clock, the bell of the house No. 35 Bogard Street was rung and upon the occupants repairing to the door to answer the call no person was to be seen, but a basket was discovered upon the steps. On taking the basket into the house, it was found to contain the living form of a white female babe, some two or three days old, with the following note pinned to its clothing: "Will the lady of this house take this infant, as it was found in the street by a colored person, and take care of it the best she can, as I suppose it has not any mother. A Friend." We are well aware that there have been great and

> important changes in the social and political relations at the South, but we never dreamt that nature had been so changed as to bring a human being into existence without a mother, and place them too in the street.[8]

By the late 1860s, facilities were increasingly inadequate throughout the South. Former Confederate men and women renewed their efforts to raise funds and provide decent care for all the state's white children. Southern orphanages remained scarce and segregated.

The Palmetto Orphan Home of South Carolina published a monthly newsletter, which included stories and notices and the constant drone of fundraising. A letter was published from a four year old during the Christmas 1873 issue: "My grandma, in Virginia, sent me 50 cents to spend as I wish. Having a dear ma to read the ORPHAN'S APPEAL to me, and hearing how many little boys and girls were giving something to you, I have concluded to send my 50 cents to the orphans." This is listed just above another notice: "D. W. Appleton of New York, who owns the land on which the city of Port Royal, in this State, is being built, has given a lot to the Palmetto Orphan Home."[9] The postbellum campaign was multifaceted, not only collecting children's allowances but also making the orphanage an integrated part of every town's landscape.

These southern philanthropists tried to work on the moral landscape as well. The ministers and town leaders felt it was not enough to build charities, but character must be built as well. The postwar reformers wanted to launch the important work of motivating people to work, to contribute to the larger goals of society.

The outreach program included a newsletter, and the Palmetto's *Orphan's Appeal* was a model of inspiration and fortitude. In one issue it reminded its readers "The poorest girls in the world are those who have never been brought up to work. There are thousands of them." Then the author goes on to warn what all too many former Confederates have learned: "The wheel of fortune rolls swiftly round—the rich are very likely to become poor, and the poor rich." And finally, the piece counsels parents, "Every daughter should be taught to earn her own living." Another story in a later issue finishes up with a confession in a jail cell: "I was a poor boy, and no one gave me a helping hand. If I had been with you in the Orphan's Home, and been taught how to gain an honest livelihood, I might have been saved from disgrace and ruin, and like you have made a noble man."[10] This is, of course, the "dying felon's" last words as he draws his final breath. Dripping with didacticism, these sugar coated offerings enticed aristocrats that they must give up drowning their sorrows (metaphorically or making literal attempts with liquor and laudanum) and develop a sweet tooth—give to charity again.

Despite all the efforts of private philanthropy and municipal funding, the extent of orphan care required state assistance. Many state governments tried to assume the burdens of dealing with the homeless and friendless. Some, like Pennsylvania, positively embraced such duties.

Over fifty thousand of Pennsylvania's 380,000 soldiers died in the war. In January 1864 Governor Andrew Gregg Curtin mounted an ambitious campaign: "I commend to the prompt attention of the Legislature the subject of the relief of poor orphans of our soldiers who have given, or shall give their lives to the country during this crisis. In my opinion their maintenance and education should be provided for by the State." In June of the same year Thomas Burrows became the state's Superintendent of Soldier's Orphans and a fifty thousand dollar donation from the Pennsylvania Railroad Company launched this effort. The state began with a modest seventy-five thousand dollar appropriation in 1865.

In 1866 the superintendent and governor planned an elaborate event, marching 345 orphans into the state capitol, to whip up support to fund the schools in the coming year.

Master George Jacobs of the McAllisterville School brought tears to his listeners' eyes with a six stanza poem:

> Oh, Legislators! Rulers! Men! around on every side
> Stand little ones whose future no tender hand will guide
> Who, powerless to help themselves, as orphan children come
> And in our martyred fathers' names, entreat of you a home.[11]

Another young boy pleaded: "Send us not back to our desolate homes ignorant and dependent as we now are. Our fathers *died for you.* Will you not educate us as a recompense for their lives?"[12] A Union General Allen vows, "This great State, which you now claim and look to as your father will not be untrue to the pledges made to him that nurtured you."[13] Finally, the governor concluded by retelling his audience about the memorable Sergeant Hamiston, found dead at Gettysburg, clutching a photograph of his three children. The sentiment and swagger of the day moved the legislators who promptly tripled the appropriation for orphan schools. And from 1870 to 1876, the average annual amount budgeted rose to over four hundred thousand dollars.

In 1876, with patriotic flourish, James Paul, the chief clerk of Pennsylvania's Department of Soldier's Orphan Schools, published a six hundred page historical tribute. This encyclopedic tome was dedicated "to the Fatherless Children of my Fallen Comrades as a Token of Esteem for the Living and a Tribute of Remembrance to the Dead." Paul proudly declared: "Let the widow and her dependent offspring become, in fact and in truth, *the children of the State,* and let the mighty people of this great Commonwealth nurture and maintain them. . . . Let us now lay the foundation of a systematic and continuous work."

A growing band of historians and social scientists have probed the ideological foundations of the welfare state and made exaggerated claims for pronouncements such as Paul's, claiming evidence of a welfare state.[14]

Whether the welfare state was in its infancy or merely a viable fetus is outside my area of expertise and interest. I won't be drawn into the debate when a cadre of agile, abracadabra scholars are hot on this trail in the wake of Theda Skocpol's influential *Protecting Soldiers and Mothers: The Political Origins of Social Policy in the United States.*[15] Although I am not particularly intrigued by theories about welfare, I am curious about the *actual* welfare of children robbed by the war machine.

Pennsylvania's well documented and extensive campaigns allow us a superb overview of the massive mobilizations to address the problems of the friendless and fatherless, motherless and homeless, as they rapidly multiplied. Relief would be made available to children of either sex under the age of fifteen who resided in Pennsylvania who were the children of deceased veterans and dependent on charity. Mothers or other guardians were required to apply for assistance. Friendless orphans under six would be placed in institutions already established within the state, while orphans over six would be sent to a particular school provided with subsidies within each of the twelve school districts.

Ironically, this plan initially met with strong resistance—as many citizens feared orphaned children would be placed in religious institutions. Once Nativist and anti-Catholic prejudice was mollified, the program worked well—perhaps too well, as soon the state had too many applications and too little money allocated to solve the growing rather than diminishing problem.

State supplements to private institutions opened floodgates, creating the impetus for dozens of charitable operations to expand or organize themselves to meet the growing need. The Philadelphia Northern Home for Friendless Children, established by benevolent women in the early 1850s, opened its doors to state wards and thus added "Soldiers' and Sailors' Orphan Institute" to its mission and its name.

Distant from this teeming urban environs, the Cassville School was built to serve the same purpose, nestled in the foothills of the Sideling Hill Mountain in a rural hamlet with three churches and four hundred residents. The graduates affectionately called themselves "sixteeners" (the age at which the state withdrew its support) and organized reunions.

The Philadelphia branch of the Freedman's Aid Society raised a complaint about the neglect of "colored orphans" in 1866. The following year the state authorized the purchase of Bristol College in Bucks County, a "commodious, and substantial brick edifice, located on the banks of the Delaware, and commanding a fine view of the river and the surrounding county."[16]

Perhaps the bucolic setting of this orphanage was a reflex response to the fact that the New York draft riots in July 1863 provoked some of the most barbaric mass violence against blacks outside the battlefield. The story of the "Burning of the Colored Orphan Asylum" was not only reported in the New York press but also syndicated in newspapers throughout the divided nation:

> As soon as the Bull's Head Hotel had been attacked by the mob, their next destination was the Colored Orphan Asylum, on Fifth Avenue, near Forty-third street. The crowd had swelled to an immense number. . . . About four hundred entered the house at the time, and immediately proceeded to pitch out beds, chairs, tables and every species of furniture, which were eagerly seized by the crowd below and carried off. When all was taken, the house was then set on fire, and shared the fate of the others. While the rioters were clamoring for admittance at the front door, the Matron and Superintendent were quietly and rapidly conducting the children out the back yard, down to the police station. . . . There were 230 children between the ages of 4 and 12 years in the home at the time of the riot.

Regardless of the motivations of its founders for anchoring this institution for African American orphans so far out in the countryside, this establishment became, in Paul's words, "the model school of the State," a thriving academy with 236 students in 1876. Paul went on to praise: "Many who have enjoyed its advantages have gone forth to fill positions of trust and usefulness. Quite a number are teaching in the South with great success. It is gratifying to know that the efforts which have been put forth in behalf of the colored soldiers' orphans have already yielded a rich harvest."[17]

Many of Paul's sketches and illustrations were meant to soothe fears about these state-run orphanages. He was particularly sensitive to any stereotype of these places as "bedlams" full of ragged, disorderly urchins. Paul lavishly detailed the order and discipline at each school. Further, he went to extraordinary lengths to offer a practical and complete outline of such mundane matters as how clothing was supplied.

At first all clothing was distributed centrally from the superintendent's office to all wards across the state. But an appropriation bill in 1871 specified that principals were allowed to purchase and distribute items through their own communities: twenty-five dollars per year allocated for ten-year-olds, younger children receiving a nineteen dollar annual clothing allowance. Careful accounts were kept of all expenditures. Principals were required to supply every child with a change of underwear and three separate sets of clothes: one each for work, school, and dress. Paul included wood cuts of a boy and a girl photographed in 1875 showing that "much taste is displayed in dressing the children." He gushes: "The boy's pants are of blue Kersey, his jacket and cap are made of dark blue cloth, trimmed with military buttons. The girl's dress is of Scotch plaid; her hat is becoming and her shoes are shapely and neat, but they do not pinch her feet."[18]

This lavish display of images, to raise both consciousness and charitable donations, was a technique popularized during the war.[19] Especially effective was a campaign launched by the American Missionary Association (AMA) in December 1863. The Union army of occupation had moved into Louisiana and established ninety-five schools with over 9,500 students, including nearly half of the black juvenile population of the state. The schools needed Yankee philanthropy to support such a massive effort, and the AMA established another five-hundred educational operations. To raise more money, they decided to send a group of eight pupils to tour photography studios in New York and Philadelphia. The sale of portraits—each labeled "the nett proceeds from the sale of these Photographs will be devoted to the education of colored people in the department of the Gulf, now under the command of Maj. Gen. Banks"—would fill empty coffers. *Harper's Weekly* reproduced the group photo, identified each child, and labeled the image: "EMANCIPATED SLAVES, WHITE AND COLORED."

The male child on stage right of the photograph was described in detail: "Charles Taylor is eight years old. His complexion is very fair, his hair light and silky. Three out of five boys in any school in New York are darker than he. Yet this white boy, with his mother, as he declares, has been twice sold as a slave. First by his father and 'owner' Alexander Wethers, of Lewis County, Virginia."

But Charles was mostly window dressing. For the centerpiece remains the light-complexioned little girls—Rebecca Huger, Rosina Downs, and Augusta Broujey—virtual starlets of the project. The girls were photographed singly and in pairs, displayed in theatrical and romanticized poses. These poses were reminiscent of images that successfully raised the sympathetic ire of northern audiences shortly before the war. Catherine S. Lawrence "redeemed" a five year old light-skinned slave child in 1860. Lawrence had the child christened in Henry Ward Beecher's church in Brooklyn. During the ceremony at Plymouth Church, Beecher held a "mock" auction, and his congregation donated the one thousand dollar purchase price of the young girl, who was nicknamed "Pinky" (Lawrence had given her the new name Fannie Virginia Cassiopeia). After the Brooklyn ceremony, Pinky was whisked to several photographers where she was dressed up like Little Red Riding Hood for one pose, in a Scottish highland outfit for another, and modeled the height of Victorian fashion in several elaborately decorated portraits, posing next to banisters, bouquets—at times with hands clasped in prayer.[20]

Her adoptive mother took her on an exhausting circuit of studios, from Brooklyn to Boston, and stopped at Hartford in between. The Lawrence portraits were an extremely

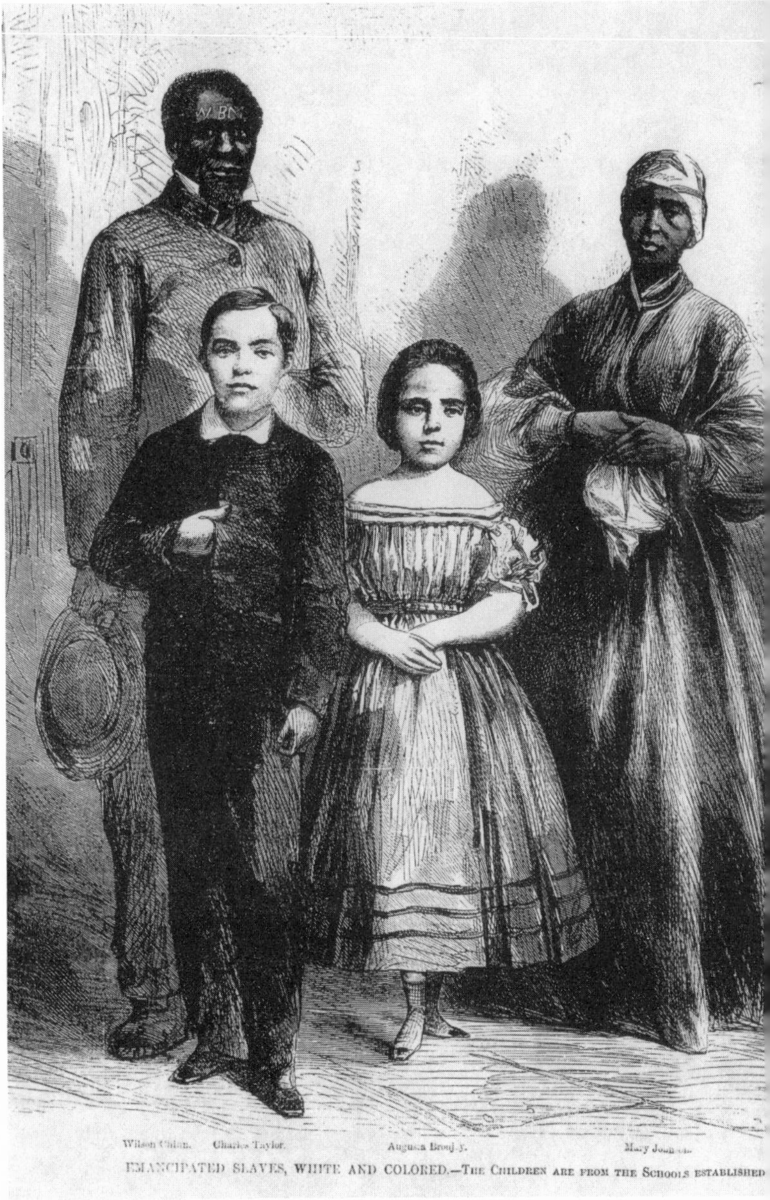
Charles Taylor.
EMANCIPATED SLAVES, WHITE AND COLORED.—The Children are from the Schools established

American Missionary Association promotion, *Harper's Weekly*, 1864.

Isaac White. Rebecca Huger. Robert Whitehead. Rosina Downs.

Orleans, by Order of Major-General Banks.—[See Page 71.]

ISAAC and ROSA, Emancipated Slave Children,
From the Free Schools of Louisiana,
Photographed by KIMBALL, 477 Broadway, N.Y.
Entered according to Act of Congress, in the year 1863 by GEO. H. HANKS, in the Clerk's Office of the U. S. for the Sou. Dist. of N.Y.

American Missionary Association studio portrait.
Courtesy of the Library of Congress.

"Redeemed" slave child.
Courtesy of the Library of Congress.

successful publicity campaign with an important commercial component. Lawrence's trial-run pioneered the popularity of the AMA fund-drive years later.

These mixed-race orphans had a peculiar status within Civil War America and pose particular challenges for historians. Their stories are difficult to discover, challenging to verify, and almost impossible to track in traditional documents available to researchers. We do have documentation of one particularly stirring tale.[21]

Sarah Grimké and her sister Angelina Grimké Weld had been firebrand feminists and abolitionists before the war. They continued their reform activities well into the war years. When Angelina discovered a notice in a paper about a young colored man named Grimké delivering an address at Lincoln University, a black college in Pennsylvania, she wrote to him to ask if he was from South Carolina (her homestate), and, if so, to tell her about himself. His reply was a revelation to the Grimké sisters:

> I am the son of Henry Grimké, a brother of Dr. John Grimké and [who is] therefore your brother. Of course you know more about my father than I do, suffice it to say he was a lawyer and was married to a Miss Simons . . . and she died leaving three children viz. Henrietta, Montague, and Thomas. After her death he took my mother, who was his slave and his children's nurse; her name is Nancy Weston. I don't think you know her, but your sister Miss Ann Grimké knows her. I heard her speak of you ladies often, especially Miss Ann. By my mother he had three children also, viz. Archibald which is my name, and Francis and John. He died about fifteen years ago, leaving my mother, with two children and in a pregnant state, for John was born two mos. after he died, in the care of his son, Mr. E. M.

> Grimké [Montague] in his own words, as I heard, "I leave Nancy and her two children to be treated as members of the family." . . . Mr. G. did not do as his father commanded.[22]

Indeed, Montague behaved vengefully toward this shadow family. He got married in 1860 and requested that Archibald be sent to his household to become his servant. When Nancy protested, he put her in jail. Archibald ran away. Frank then left and became a valet to a Confederate soldier. After two years, Archibald was recognized while stationed in Charleston then put in a workhouse. His half-brother Montague then sold him to another officer. John was sold away as well. The brothers were only reunited after the Confederate surrender. Archibald and Frank's education at Lincoln University had been sponsored by the philanthropist Parker Pillsbury. Archibald concluded, "Perhaps you would like to see our pictures, they are enclosed. I shall hope to hear from you soon."

The most common response would have been not to reply at all. On rare occasion, the white family member might have sent a check. But in this unique case, Angelina Grimké not only responded warmly, but announced her intention of visiting soon. Both Angelina and Sarah contributed to the support of these newly discovered nephews, and Angelina attended their graduation exercises at Lincoln, taking her son Stuart Weld with her.

Archibald's brother, Frank Grimké, attended Princeton Theological Seminary, and assumed the pulpit at a church in Washington where he remained for almost half a century. In 1878, he married writer Charlotte Forten, from a comfortable Philadelphia free black family, who had been a teacher in Port Royal, South Carolina, during the war.

Archibald earned a law degree from Harvard in 1874 and

settled in Boston. He wrote biographies of William Lloyd Garrison and Charles Sumner, scholarship that would have endeared him to his activist aunts if they had lived to see his career blossom. He became an American consulate to Santo Domingo and served as a vice-president of the NAACP, earning the Spingarn medal in 1919 for lifetime achievement. These remarkable boys, orphaned to face the cruel consequences of slavery's sexual double standard, were set adrift by war and could have joined the millions of freedpeople denied opportunity by poverty and racism. But they were united with their remarkable aunts. So the Grimké sisters (at least the two of them who were pioneer reformers) became remarkable role models for the next generation of Grimké brothers (the African American brothers, who survived the harshness of slavery, war, and abandonment), and Angelina Weld Grimké, the poet, was a product of this blended family in its next generation.

Another remarkable tale involving African American orphans can be gleaned from a heroic saga, played out remarkably on the plantations of the Confederate President Jefferson Davis.[23] In rural Mississippi before the Civil War, Benjamin T. Montgomery was a gifted man, admired by his fellow slaves as an inventor, a machinist, but most of all, a leader. Montgomery convinced his owner, Joseph Davis, the brother of Jefferson Davis, that he could manage not only the planting operations but a plantation store as well. Davis liberally agreed, as he was a radical on the subject of slave management. Profits from the operation meant that income allowed Montgomery's wife, also a slave, to remain at home to raise the four surviving of their five children, a luxury denied all but a handful of bondswomen.

With the outbreak of the Civil War, the Montgomery family escaped to Cincinnati, but they returned to Mississippi after Lee's surrender. General Ulysses S. Grant, who had visited Davis Bend during the war, predicted it could be "a negro paradise." Montgomery boldly took out a mortgage on those lands formerly belonging to the Davis family. Montgomery organized a black tenant operation that flourished under his direction. This African American community established self-government, electing their own sheriffs and judges. Benjamin Montgomery, not surprisingly, served as justice of the peace.

Montgomery's wife, Mary Lewis, initiated her own planting operation on 130 acres—employing orphaned children whom she had taken into her household. Her Home Farm gained national fame when she produced the "best bale of cotton" at the 1870 St. Louis Fair and later at the Philadelphia Centennial in 1876.

We know little about these black orphans beyond their names and their majestic accomplishments, but it shows that many African Americans managed without government assistance and employed techniques of self reliance, as long as the forces of federal Reconstruction were in place to insure African Americans opportunity. It also demonstrates that within black families following the war, many black children were taken in simply as a matter of course. Frances Rollin of South Carolina, born to free black parents in Charleston before the war, knew when she married William Whipper she would not only be expected to raise his child by blood, his son Buddy, but Demps Powell, a young black boy who had been Whipper's sidekick during the war and was also considered a part of the family. The oral histories and family memoirs of African Americans are overflowing with these stories of adoption, which continue the tradition of "fictive kin" developed within slave communities. Many Africans on the ships over to America found themselves bereft of family by blood but would form close ties with those from their village or simply those with whom they were sold, to form "fictive," but just as enduring, kinship ties. For many African Americans, apparently the Civil War provided a similar catalyst.

For black and white Americans alike, the war was a wrenching time of dislocation. The Civil War tore communities and families apart. The dimensions of this trauma and destruction have been chronicled by many scholars and writers, many genealogists and archivists, but perhaps there are always more dramas to uncover, more tales to tell within this fascinating panorama.

Certainly the records of the Freedman's Bureau Papers have become a rich resource for family history, renewed and restored through the efforts of a team of scholars producing volumes that offer greater appreciation of the complexities of blacks' postwar experience. These edited collections allow increasing and populist access to these compelling documents.[24] Some scholars are beginning to use other kinds of documentary sources to trace the ways in which African Americans tried to reconstitute families after the war, reuniting parents and children, orphaned siblings, and others.[25]

Stephen Oates's recent biography of Clara Barton, *Woman of Valor*,[26] highlights her postwar work on behalf of missing soldiers. Even before the Civil War concluded, Barton recognized that the problem of locating loved ones would be an enormous challenge in the wake of prison deaths, unmarked graves, and refugee families. Barton established a clearinghouse for tracing lost soldiers at Annapolis. This task propelled her into a controversial tangle of issues and a collision course with certain branches of government bureaucracy.

Her search for missing federal soldiers naturally led to Andersonville, the notorious Confederate prison where so many Union prisoners lost their lives. She traveled to Georgia in the Summer of 1865 to help identify remains and rebury the dead—in essence to assure several thousand children that, sadly, they were indeed orphans.

Despite her heroic efforts, Barton was not appointed head of a Bureau of Missing Persons but increasingly became at odds with the War Department. Having fought military red tape her entire career, Barton sidestepped the chain of command and launched a private crusade from her headquarters—taking her campaign to the newspapers, printing circulars with lists of missing men, reaching out directly to anxious families. She gained a powerful ally with the support of newspaper editor Horace Greeley.

Barton's work stirred up enormous passion. She was able to locate information on dying men by soliciting the testimony of soldiers who witnessed a comrade's death, so details could be conveyed to families in agonizing limbo. Barton sifted through Confederate records to uncover burial information on thousands, forwarding information to the loved ones of those who perished in prison. By providing these family members with vital details, Barton's work both put to rest the awful sense of not knowing what happened to men sent off to war as well as supplied many with information necessary to secure pensions.

Congress finally recognized the significance of Barton's campaign and appropriated fifteen thousand dollars for her work. By the time she closed down her operation in 1869, Barton had exhausted all the government's money and nearly two thousand dollars from her own pocket. Barton herself went without salary as she and her staff processed over sixty-three thousand inquiries, providing more than twenty-two thousand families with information on missing soldiers. It was only through Barton's heroic efforts that many families were finally able to bury their dead and move on with their lives.

In addition to the thousands of letters Barton fielded, the Records of the Office of the Adjunct General, Enlisted Branch, housed at the National Archives, contain box after box of additional letters to the government filled with correspondence begging for information on missing soldiers. (I have labeled these as "Lost Boys" in my own files—and they are sobering and engrossing to read—handkerchief as well as notecards are required.)

A sampling from 1863 reveals women desperate for any help they can get, many utterly destitute:

- Emeline Hermance of Troy wrote to President Lincoln on June 15 without her son's knowledge, begging that her oldest child (who enlisted at seventeen although she "never signed the paper") be released—as she had "young children to support." She also added, "If this son should fall in battle I feel that it would crush me."[27]
- Bridget Heart, a widow from Ireland, wrote on July 26, begging any news of her son, who she hadn't heard from since February 1862.[28]
- Mary Herrick wrote to the government on May 30 to beg for the discharge of her son from the army: "I can pray for peace once more to fold his blessed wings around us and return each son to his dessolate mother."[29]

Most mothers had to remain desolate, as Lincoln, Secretary of War Stanton, and commanding officers rarely granted requests for discharge, no matter how wretched and desperate families left behind were. And requests for information were usually met with little or no satisfaction until Clara Barton stepped in with her massive operations.

There are many, many examples of individual heart rending tales of orphans—some known, but most nameless victims of war. However, I am going to close with some thoughts about a girl named Rose. While working on this project, I wondered which of the many tales of the white South I might choose to include in this venue. How could I pick just one example, and what emblem might be most appropriate for *Civil War Stories?* I was startled by the revelation offered on the cover of one of my previous books, *Tara Revisited: Women, War, and the Plantation Legend.* There she was on the cover: Rose O'Neal Greenhow. Yes, of course we know the heroic tale of the Confederate spy who died in the service of her country. But as I stared into the photograph, I realized what I needed to see was beyond the glory and into the grief and loss, which was staring back at me, reflected in the eyes of a little girl: Rose Greenhow's daughter and namesake, with whom Greenhow posed in her most famous portrait outside "Fort Greenhow," as her guarded home became known. (Because of the identical mother-daughter name, I will refer to the daughter as "young Rose.")

Young Rose had suffered with her mother every step of the way, except for death by drowning while trying to run the blockade. Her mother's demise was heroic, but what about the little girl who had suffered for her country, was deprived, imprisoned, and subjected to punishment cruel and unusual by any standard but most especially for an eight-year-old girl? Because of her mother's heroism, Rose became a motherless orphan, another victim of war.

Rose O'Neal herself was orphaned at an early age, when her father, a Maryland planter, was killed by his African

Rose Greenhow and her daughter Rose.
Courtesy of the Library of Congress.

American valet in 1817. O'Neal left his daughters money and land. When Rose's sister made an excellent match with James Cutts, Dolley Madison's nephew, Rose obtained direct and easy access to elite Washington society. After Rose wed the Virginia lawyer Robert Greenhow in 1835, she bore, in rapid succession, four daughters: Florence, Gertrude, Leila, and her youngest, Rose. The couple was a glittering fixture on the national social scene. And when Robert Greenhow died in 1854, his widow continued her prominent role as a society hostess. Rumor abounded that she never lacked male companionship.

Rose Greenhow was a great favorite of President Buchanan, the only bachelor elected to the presidency. She was a confidante of Buchanan's niece and White House hostess, Harriet Lane. During the sectional debates of the late 1850s, especially following John Brown's raid in 1859, Rose entertained fire-eaters and Yankee abolitionists. She courted powerful men on both sides of the aisle, who represented both North and South, although her sympathies were decidedly Confederate. Rose Greenhow became very close, allegedly intimate, with Senator Henry Wilson of Massachusetts, a strong antislavery advocate. Letters were found in her home wrapped in ribbon with the notation "Letters from H not to be opened—but burn in case of death or accident." They were later seized by the government during a raid on her home and ended up on file at the War Department, embarrassing the gentleman who had written to the object of his affection and reputed mistress on Senate stationery.

Rose suspended her social activities in December 1860 when her daughter Gertrude fell ill. Rose was devastated when her daughter died the next year in March. She might have gone to visit her other daughter Florence in California, who was expecting a child, had Greenhow not been so deeply involved in an espionage ring—studying ciphers and message drops, trafficking in military information and coded letters.

With the outbreak of war, Greenhow and her southern comrades were under surveillance—by Pinkerton agents. Despite her warm relations with prominent Unionists, the forty-four-year-old widow was placed under house arrest on August 23, 1861, when it was rightfully suspected that she had passed on vital information concerning Union troops before Manassas (Bull Run). Mary Chesnut had commented that Greenhow gathered her "secessionist dames" to do sewing: "It gives a quaint look, the twinkling of needles, and the ever-lasting sock dangling. A Jury of Matrons, so to speak, sat at Mrs. Greenhow's. They say Mrs. Greenhow furnished Beauregard with the latest information of the Federal movements, and so made the Manassas victory a possibility. She sent us the enemy's plans. Everything she said proved true, numbers, route and all."[30]

Fort Greenhow remained home to Rose and her eight-year-old daughter, Rose, as well as several other Washington women, including Eugenia Phillips, a Jewish society hostess, and Ellie Poole, a correspondent for both the *Richmond Enquirer* and the *Baltimore Exchange.* Federal authorities subjected these women to round-the-clock guards. Greenhow objected strenuously, as federals incarcerated shady characters in her home. She was appalled by a "Mrs. Onderdunk," a woman "of bad repute and recognized by . . . the guard as such, having been seen . . . in the exercises of her vocation."[31]

On November 17, Rose wrote to Secretary of State Seward indignant about her seizure: "And thus for a period of seven days, I, with my little child, was placed absolutely at the mercy of men without character or responsibility; that during the first evening a portion of these men became brutally drunk and boasted in my hearing of the *nice times* they expected to have with the female prisoners, and that rude violence was used towards a servant girl during that first evening."[32] She scribbled and complained incessantly about her daughter Rose: "My poor little girl was circumscribed to a few feet in front of the house, with an extra guard detached to watch her."[33]

Greenhow was outraged by the whimsical way her captors treated her: "On Saturday, January 18 at two o'clock, I learned incidentally, that I was to be moved from my own house to another prison. I was sitting in the library reading, with my little one at my feet playing with her dolls, prattling, and beguiling me almost into forgetfulness of the wickedness and persecutions which beset me, until recalled by this startling intelligence. . . . The few articles of clothing for myself and child, which I was allowed to take, were gathered together and packed, with a sentinel standing over, and examining each piece separately. Less than two hours was allowed me, before I was dragged from my home for ever."[34]

Prison life was even more ghastly as she recorded in a diary: "January 28: Today the dinner for myself and child consists of a bowl of beans swimming in grease, two slices of fat junk, and two slices of bread." Two days later, Greenhow complained: "My child has been ill for several days, brought on by close confinement and want of proper food." She finally confessed: "I became now seriously alarmed about the health and life of my child. Day by day I saw her fading away—her round chubby face, radiant with health, had become pale as marble, the pupils of her eyes were unnaturally dilated, and finally a slow nervous fever seized upon her. I implored in vain, both verbally and in writing, that a physician might be sent."[35]

Apparently, the federal authorities were engaged in a battle of wills—intent to break Rose's spirit, even if they had to employ young Rose to do it. In March 1862 Greenhow was taken to what she thought was a kangaroo court, where she tested the patience of her Union inquisitors. Greenhow angrily denied false reports about her in the press. She even went so far as to write from her jail cell to the editor of the *Baltimore News* in early April: "I have made no confession of treason, or treasonable correspondence; neither was I subjected to an examination intended to bring to the light my sources of information. I but claim the right which our fathers did in '76—to protest against tyranny and oppression."[36] But by May, even the Union knew that this war of nerves between mother and daughter and the federal authorities could not last much longer, as Rose reported: "My child is so nervous from a repetition of these dreadful scenes [a prisoner was shot] that she starts and cries out in her sleep. Horror like this will shatter the nerves of the strongest."[37]

When Rose and her daughter were released into Virginia on June 2, the *Richmond Dispatch* jubilantly declared: "If the tyrant has released her, it was because that even he quailed before the might of her power as representative of the feelings of every true Southern lady."[38] Indeed, Rose proudly reported that she refused to mix with other female prisoners, unless they were her social equals—exercising snobbery under the most dire and humbling conditions.

Greenhow was given a patriotic homecoming in Richmond. Jefferson Davis praised her role in the victory at Bull Run, and she was overcome with pride. Greenhow continued her intelligence work and volunteered to undertake assignments abroad.

In August 1863, she set sail for Europe, an emissary for Davis. Here Greenhow was running the blockade, although never having been abroad before. This truly fearless woman was praised by Douglas Southall Freeman: "Her proud loyalty to the South and her will and courage set her apart as a woman who would welcome death from a firing squad if it would serve her cause."[39]

Rose was ostensibly making this journey to put her youngest daughter in a convent school—out of harm's way and nearer to her older sister Florence, who was living in London. Leila was stashed in a boarding school in Pennsylvania. After Rose's difficult ordeal, especially harrowing to be imprisoned with her child, she enjoyed her new social opportunities abroad. As Davis's delegate, she was presented to both Napoleon III and Queen Victoria. While in London, Greenhow published *My Imprisonment and the First Year of Abolition Rule at Washington* to promote support of the Rebel cause.

On her return voyage to the Confederacy, Greenhow was smuggling both gold and secret documents when her ship ran aground near the North Carolina shore. She wore a leather reticule on a long chain containing two thousand dollars in gold and three hundred sovereigns, with some coins sewn into her clothing. It was imperative to get both the money and the documents to Jefferson Davis. Greenhow forced the ship's captain to give her and two other Confederate agents a rowboat so they could reach land and avoid capture. Instead, their small vessel was hit by a large wave and capsized shortly after they shoved off. Rose alone drowned, weighed down by her personal cargo of gold and documents. Her body was taken to Wilmington where she lay in state with a military guard. Shops were closed in honor of her passing. Her coffin was draped with the Confederate flag. Hundreds came to mourn Greenhow at her funeral, the greatest Confederate heroine ever imaginable: a woman who literally gave her life for her country.

While Confederates mourned their fallen heroine at her state funeral, her three surviving daughters grieved privately. Greenhow had given herself to the Confederacy, but her daughters, none able to attend the funeral, had lost their mother long before. Perhaps young Rose was the child who suffered the most.

Young Rose remained in the convent until she was seventeen. American friends accompanied her back to the States so she could live with her sister Florence and her brother-in-law, Gen. Tradwell Moore, who had worked his way up U.S. Army ranks to become the commandant at Newport. In Rhode Island young Rose fell madly in love with West Point graduate Lt. William Penn Duvall and they wed in haste. The marriage did not last, as Duvall was a strict, rigid disciplinarian who objected to his wife's "flightiness" and eventually divorced her.

On her own again, Rose Greenhow Duvall next went on the stage, but only for a brief stint.[40] It was as though she could only endure being featured as Rose Greenhow, withstanding her memories, to cash in on fame for just a fleeting moment. And this episode may have brought about her total collapse, as shortly after retirement from the stage, Rose Greenhow Duvall returned to France, withdrew from public life, and devoted herself to the Catholic Church. She exiled herself from her homeland, her memories, and the secular world entirely.

I have discovered no accounts with young Rose's version of events. We know she could not have been happy to lose her mother at such a tender age, even as a contribution to the glorious Confederate cause. We know that she began her life in the cradle of the American aristocracy, pampered by her mother's White House friends. Then war intervened—and nothing would ever be the same again.

Rose Greenhow, the Confederate spy, was but one among millions who suffered and were deprived during wartime—and but one of thousands who lost their lives. Yet she was a *rebel* in every sense of the word. She defied the dictates of society to perform courageously within a Washington spy ring. Under surveillance and house arrest, Greenhow kept her cool and probably saved thousands of her countrymen's lives by her nerve and bravado. She went abroad as an ambassador for the Confederate cause. She was the only woman known to die in the line of duty. She became a martyr for her country. Yet, looking back over historical accounts, her celebrity and heroism was not as exalted as one might expect in the postwar South.

This was due in part to the Yankees who besmirched Greenhow's virtue—those scandalous letters from "Senator H" were hard to interpret in any but the most compromising light. This rather lurid liaison contributed to Rose's role being minimized within Confederate lore for many years. She defied the rules of southern ladyhood, which convinced Confederate males to downplay her career as an agent. It would be several generations before this patriot, who may have used whatever means necessary to coax Union men into revealing state secrets, gained serious reconsideration. Greenhow's ambiguous legacy and her compromised reputation may have had a profound impact on her namesake, who retreated from a secular life and devoted herself to Catholicism and its tenets. Young Rose must have been aware that her mother had allegedly abandoned celibacy and purity, forsaking church perhaps for state.

Rose Greenhow risked her reputation and eventually her life. She was one of a handful of women who became involved in dangerous wartime espionage and one of the few mothers to take on such a role. She gambled and lost all for her country. Looking at the mother-daughter portrait, her face is stoic, composed, refined, and determined.

Shifting our gaze to young Rose, we detect her pale reflection—a brave girl, and yet so innocent of the costs, of which her mother must have been recklessly aware. With hindsight, looking into young Rose's eyes, we can see a glimmer of her sorrow stretching ahead, an ache of loss shared by thousands. And all of this pain was rarely diminished by patriotic rhetoric.

Orphans were taught to revere their lost loved ones and to take pride in the sacrifice departed parents made, not only for their country but also for their children's future. Their "homelessness" is a neglected but nevertheless noble element of the Civil War's epic sadness.[41]

The great ship of state weathered the worst storm in its history, a tropical gale of fierce and bitter dimensions. Battered and leaking, the vessel barely made it back to port in one piece. But it did. Those who rode out the storm at sea, and those who worried and waited back on land, longed to celebrate the national triumph of homecoming, the promise of return. Homelessness was all but forgotten.

But now we must set ourselves a new course in Civil War studies, to revisit those faces, those moments, those tributes and try to imagine a whole sea of children, lining the docks, waving us back—beckoning us to tell stories, *their* stories of war.

CHAPTER THREE

Legendary Valor

South Carolina Women Reconstruct the War

FOLLOWING CONFEDERATE SURRENDER IN THE Spring of 1865, Charleston, the cradle of secessionism, confronted one of its most daunting challenges—to simultaneously acknowledge the past and face the future. How the era from 1861 to 1865 would be reflected in history books launched a new kind of campaign, one in which citizens, black and white, male and female, engaged to preserve a legacy for future generations.

The dimensions of this protracted conflict are still with us today as we move forward toward a new century and an even *newer* New South, grappling with the dilemmas of race relations, power shifts, economic upheavals. We still struggle with shared and segregated meanings of victories and defeats over the past two centuries of South Carolina's past. My goal is to tell stories that allow us to move beyond the simple recounting of wins and losses, the litany of events. I want us to discover the way in which storytellers in the past have significantly shaped our future with their competing agendas, creating a contest of words as well as wills, ensnaring those of us committed to exploring southern history.

Usually when we explore the glory days of war we think of men in battle, but my subjects today will be those women who struggled over the even greater debate of the history of the war. The pair of women I chose to highlight seems as ideal a duo as I might want to find: women whose struggles in postwar South Carolina capture, each in her own way, the saga of Reconstruction. My female warriors took up not swords but their pens, each committed to her patriotic duty to promote the best interests of her people—to counter the crippling effects of postwar decline.

I will begin with the wartime experiences of the Louisa

Cheves McCord family. McCord's story is better known than that of her daughter whose writing I spotlight, but the famous mother provided the crucial backstory that shaped her daughter's destiny in the postwar era.[1] Louisa Cheves was born the daughter of Langdon Cheves, a powerful South Carolina politician and jurist. In 1840 Louisa Cheves married widower David McCord when she was nearly thirty and he was forty-three. Politician and planter, David McCord had been widowed only a few months, and his wife left behind their eight children. But Louisa's marriage was, by all measures, a love match—not simply McCord seeking a stepmother, as several of the children were farmed out to relatives upon their father's remarriage. Within months of their wedding, David and Louisa had their own child, Langdon Cheves McCord (known as Cheves), followed by two daughters, Hannah and Louisa.

The unmarried Louisa Cheves had been precocious and a favorite of her father's. (Louisa's daughter and namesake followed in her mother's footsteps, as she recalled: "My Father was a trustee of the South Carolina college and as such kept a key to the library. Many of my young days were spent in the library with him, poring over the illustrated books while he read.")[2]

Louisa McCord was a veritable bluestocking compared to many in her circle. The brilliant young woman spent her twenties as the capable daughter of an invalid mother and absentee planter before moving on to her role as plantation mistress, wife, and mother. During her thirties, she blossomed as a writer, encouraged by her husband to publish her political and fictional compositions. After fifteen years of marriage, McCord's husband died in the Spring of 1855. Louisa was emotionally devastated but prepared to assume responsibility for her own children and their welfare. Indeed, David Mc-Cord, aware of his wife's impending inheritance, had left all his property to his children by his first marriage.

Louisa barely had time to recover from the loss of her husband when she was saddled with the care of her ailing father. These nursing duties were strenuous and psychologically stressful—to care for the man from whom she had drawn her strength, a man felled by illness only months after she lost her beloved husband. Louisa's father died in 1857. During this period, her own health deteriorated and she sought a cure in Europe, taking Cheves and Louisa along, while her other daughter remained behind. The family was reunited in South Carolina in 1859 and watched as secessionist crises rapidly escalated into war. By this time, due to her husband's supportive influence and her own indomitable spirit, Louisa McCord was a nationally recognized literary figure—a poet and playwright. She was an accomplished essayist as well and her political writing revealed her to be a staunch advocate of states' rights, an articulate champion of southern exceptionalism.

By the time the war broke out Louisa had already lost the two most important men in her life: her father and her husband. Yet she did not shrink from her patriotic duty and embraced the role of Roman matron. McCord sent her only son off to war—to fight for the Confederacy. Indeed, when Cheves McCord was made a captain, she personally donated supplies and uniforms to outfit his entire company—and encouraged other patriots to follow her example. She remained an impassioned supporter of the rebellion. Her fellow South Carolinian, Mary Boykin Chesnut, applauded her example: "Mrs. McCord scorns whispers, and speaks out. She says:

These are our soldiers. Since the world began there were never better. . . . The real ammunition of our war is faith in ourselves and enthusiasm in our cause."[3]

The donation of her son, the invasion and occupation of her home, and the defeat of the Confederate cause were crushing blows to the staunch secessionist, Louisa Cheves McCord. The sufferings and losses seemed insurmountable at the time. But Louisa's youngest daughter sought to triumph over all this tragedy by resurrecting the memory of her fallen brother and her family's devotion to the Lost Cause with the publication of Louisa McCord Smythe's *For Old Lang Syne: Collected for My Children,* privately published in Charleston. (Lang Syne was the Cheves family plantation, a gift of Langdon to his daughter Louisa, and a gift of Louisa McCord to her daughter Louisa and Louisa's husband Augustine Smythe.)

A typescript transcription of the original manuscript was donated by a McCord descendent, Harriet Popham McDougall, to the South Carolina Historical Society in 1979. This generous gesture allows historians to recover missing pages of history that all too often end up in dustbins or destroyed accidentally. When I came across the Smythe document, I was already fascinated by this particular genre of southern women's writings. In *Tara Revisited: Women, War, and the Plantation Legend,* I discuss the blossoming of the white southern woman's war memoirs at the turn of the century. Certainly dozens were undertaken as family projects, most privately published, but by the time southern and northern soldiers were united by a common enemy in the Spanish-American War, the general public was eager for the "befo' the woh" genre of southern reminiscences. Virginia Clay Clopton, Myrta Lockett Avary, and several other triple-named southern women took the literary market by storm with their autobiographical literature.

Northern audiences had been softened by decades of southern tales of white suffering, especially in the short story fiction market that was burgeoning by the 1890s. From the period following the war until the mid-1880s, most southern authors idealized the antebellum period and portrayed the years after the war as the dark ages enforced by Yankee occupation. From E. A. Pollard's *The Lost Cause* (1866) on through to the modern era, a steady stream of romantic, sentimentalized portrayals appeared.

Mary Boykin Chesnut's posthumously published diary appeared in 1906, edited by Isabella Martin and Myrta Lockett Avary. These propagandistic memoirs were meant to blur the lines of embitterment. They were sentimental embellishments aimed at binding the nation back together—the "belle tells all" school of plantation studies.

These colorful revisionist texts are full of bluster. Eliza Ripley proclaimed in her reminiscences of antebellum Louisiana: "I am no apologist for slavery: the whites suffered more from its demoralizing influence than the blacks, but we were born to it, grew up with it, lived with it and it was our daily life. We did well by it; no people could have done better. It is past now."[4]

What is past is past, but what is past is prologue and remained a stubborn roadblock to reform. So many of these literary products were not-so-subtle propaganda meant to rose-tint the past and to vilify the present. Efforts to create racial reform were hampered by such romanticism.

I do not mean to belittle these publishing efforts, rather I want to take them seriously as a literary genre, in a way I think they have been previously dismissed. I hope to complete a study of these autobiographical texts at some future time, furnishing excerpts and commentary, entitled "Remembrance of Things Imagined."

At the same time, I find most of these volumes formulaic and predictable. Indeed, their predictability leads me to the conclusion that most neo-Confederate authors promoted a party line, especially on the thorny question of race. Unfortunately, the party line on race becomes criss-crossed by contradictory evidence. Postbellum white women faced the mounting challenge of whitewashing the peculiar institution of the New South: lynching. Jim Crow was one thing, snaking its way into everyday life, eroding the hard fought inroads of black equality during the postwar era. But racially motivated ritual murder was splashing its way into national headlines, a blood sport of southern bigotry tarnishing the region's good name.

So it is my contention that a literature of apology materialized. This literature had a simple mission that became tremendously successful. These plantation recollections were intended to conjure a romanticized portrait of prewar harmony. Smythe does not fail in this regard. Indeed, the first few pages of the manuscript are devoted almost entirely to her nostalgia for former slaves. Smythe begins with a familiar gambit: "I have often promised you children—the older ones I mean—to write something for you about when I was a little girl. But the days and years have slipped by and not one word has been set down until now, when a quiet afternoon with nobody in the house has set me to thinking of the old days."[5] She spends her opening pages on the devotion and antics of Maum Di, Maum Kate, Maum Rache, Daddy Jack, and others, confess-

The family of Louisa McCord Smythe, for whom she wrote her memoir. Courtesy of Eliza Cleveland.

ing: "I have as you know the greatest weakness in my heart for old darkeys. If I indulge in many reminiscences of the old folks it won't hurt you to read them for you are destined never to see their like."[6]

This is a constant theme of the plantation memoir, that former slaves were loyal, devoted, irreplaceable. Smythe argues repeatedly that McCord slaves were exemplary: "To the credit of the negroes be it said that they were perfectly kind and respectful through these terrible days and did their best for us, as they had done all through the war."[7] I do not wish to debate this point in any evidentiary manner, rather to reflect on both the legends and the valor highlighted in Louisa McCord Smythe's text—to tease out the political intent emblematic within Confederate women's memoirs.

It is key to understanding her appreciation of the loyalty of her former slaves that she saw it as a testimony to her family's accomplishments, as Smythe explained, "their self control was indeed a high compliment to those who had trained and taught them for generations and was the best possible contradiction to the theory of their past sufferings."[8]

Here Smythe defends her class against claims of cruelty and abuse, and she further asserts:

> They certainly now had every opportunity for revenge. None however was taken, but deluded, poor creatures, by false promises, frightened by the sight of those to whom they had looked for everything in such absolute need, and no doubt feeling themselves the pinching of our poverty as they had felt the comfort of our plenty; they one by one began to disappear from the yards of their former owners. Where they went, why or when they went, no one knew. Simply when called they did not appear, and in many instances never appeared again, to *our* eyes at least.[9]

Now the creeping dissemblance that characterizes these white women's recollections begins to emerge. How is it that a happy contented people ran off for unknown reasons to parts unknown, or perhaps lurked just out of sight?

Smythe struggled with her own ambivalence, in the moment and in her recollections, as she went on to rationalize: "At first this was a relief, though a sad one. The thought of fewer mouths to fill . . . was a comfort, but as the thing went on it became *ludicrously inconvenient* [emphasis added]."[10]

Now we get at the crux of the issue—the inconvenience of disappearing slaves, for at the outset of the war, Smythe confided: "Fortunately for us there were still plenty of servants to mend our clothes."[11] So the loyalty of African Americans is an economic necessity as much as political propaganda for former slaveholders. Confederate matrons still saw African Americans as labor commodities, not just status symbols.

Clearly the white women left behind during wartime had more to contend with than ambivalence. They were expected to keep the home fires burning, to maintain not only plantation households stripped of white males but also to donate goods to Confederate soldiers desperately in need of food, clothing, and medical supplies. These burdens were enormous. And many women less steely than McCord despaired when trying to equip the army *and* sustain the swelling bands of refugees while supplies dwindled and demands skyrocketed.

Yet the phrasing "ludicrous inconvenience" betrays class views, as when Smythe complained that her slaves had to stand in long lines to receive rations from supply wagons. This is not to say that the McCord family did not suffer much more than mere "inconvenience." Indeed, Smythe's tale turns harrowing when she recounts preparing for the "worst": Sherman's arrival.

The family buries the silver, stockpiles supplies, boards up the pantry, watches others flee, and soon the town is under siege. A swarm of men in coonskin caps breaks into the house. After Louisa McCord confronted them, a

> wretch caught her by the throat and jerked the watch out of her dress with such force that he broke the leather. Either he or one of the others—it must have been another one—had all of

> our knives gathered in sheaves in his hands, and shook them in her face. Poor aunt Rachel retreated. . . . She almost fell into the room, white and faint, calling "Oh, girls they are killing your mother." . . . What might have happened I don't know, but just as the man was pushing past my mother, the door bell rang. She said the men stopped instantly which she noticed, so when it rang again she said just on the chance "there are some of your officers and you had better not let them find you here." In one minute they were gone! Just like a flight of vultures.[12]

The flight of vultures was only the beginning, as Smythe recounted tumultuous and appalling tales of arson, starvation, and occupation. The fear and ransacking took a terrible toll, and the family was left in shambles. This tragic encounter is also part of the "damn Yankee" genre of Confederate historiography.

But perhaps the most striking and iconographic feature of Smythe's memoir is her description of her brother's death and glory. Her weaving together her mother's loss, the family's sacrifice, and the devotion of Cheves's manservant provides a melancholy tale with near Shakespearean dimensions. Smythe describes her brother's prompt enlistment and her mother's lavish send-off, as the hopes and fears of the entire family march off to war with this lone male descendent. Family folklore exalts the young Cheves, as his sister reported:

> Some of the young fellows were a little sore with their gentlemanly ideas at being ordered to this kind of work. They said they had volunteered as soldiers, not as laborers, and fight they would, but work that way they would not. The officer in command—Capt. Chicester I think—was rather in a quandary. Insubordination could not be allowed and yet he was loath to pro-

> ceed to extreme measures. . . . His relief can be imagined when Capt. Cheves without a word loaded a wheelbarrow and quickly bundled it up the plank before the eyes of the rebellious. In a minute the trouble was over—all hands were at work without a murmur.[13]

McCord's nobility is further exemplified by an additional anecdote: "I have a letter from my brother to my mother thanking her for a supply of Quinine she had sent him, but saying that it would be impossible for him to take it as there was not enough for all, and he was not willing to take less risks than the men did. Such was the spirit of our boys."[14]

So the noble, self-sacrificing young Confederate captain ascended the pedestal. He was wounded in battle, suffering a head injury and temporarily crippled by gunshot wounds to his foot and leg. Upon his return home, the family hailed him as a hero: "We had a wheeled chair for him, and round and round the garden, and round the campus he would go with one of his willing, worship slaves [his sisters] pushing him while the rest followed."[15] Cheves was recuperating at home when a military physician arrived to extract the bullet from his head—and succeeded. Louisa Smythe went on to describe: "Mamma entreated him to ask for ten days more, but he refused, saying that Dr. Horlbeck had performed the operation and knew his condition and told him to go—he *could* not ask for delay."[16]

What followed was heart wrenching to his family. Cheves returned to the army, writing home about forced marches and ghastly conditions, "of no food but the corn gathered from the fields and eaten raw—one day there was *no* food, but their poor old haversacks were so greasy that they kept themselves up by sucking the corners."[17] Shortly thereafter,

Captain McCord collapsed and died before his mother could reach him. His body was accompanied home by his body servant Tom.

The family was engulfed by their grief. Cheves left behind a wife and child. Louisa McCord lost her only son. Louisa Smythe recalled the poignant burial tableaux: "I remember my poor Mother falling on her knees at the open grave, and dropping into it as a last token, one of her gloves, I have the match now; she had never parted with it."[18]

Louisa McCord convinced her nephew Willie Haskell to take his cousin Cheves's watch with him when he returned to military duty. It was soon returned when Haskell perished on the killing fields at Gettysburg. Soon after, Louisa McCord lost her brother Langdon as well. Despite all these setbacks, McCord remained devoted to the Confederate cause, as Mary Chesnut reported: "Spent to-day with Mrs. McCord at her hospital. She is dedicating her grief for her son, sanctifying it, one might say, by giving up her soul and body, her days and nights, to the wounded soldiers at her hospital. Every moment of her time is surrendered to their needs."[19]

The sacrifices of Louisa McCord are rendered even more sympathetic in her daughter's tale of her brother's deification. One of the most stylized passages within the memoir includes both Langdon Cheves McCord's elevation to sainthood and the process of memorialization that followed:

> The little coal we had was saved and doled out to keep alive the flowers in the greenhouse. They were so associated with your Uncle Cheves who was a great lover of flowers that we could not bear to let them go. After his death, his man Tom returned to his old place as gardener and through all the trouble the garden and greenhouse were kept as though their young master

> and lover were expected to come back to them. But at last the day came when Tom had to say that there was only coal enough to make the fire once more! It was a bitter cold evening, and I well remember the look on Mamma's face and on poor Tom's as she said, "Well, Tom, keep it up as long as you can." The fire was lit but burned out before morning and in a day or two our dear flowers were nothing but blackened sticks. The doors of the two greenhouses were locked and we left them like graves. I never entered them again.[20]

This is a very symbolic portrait. After all, was it likely that coal was doled out to keep the flowers alive when families were cold and starving across the South? The image of sacrifice and gentility is central to Smythe's narrative and to the glorious tales of Confederate lore. Within these fables, both whites and blacks share the privilege of honoring the fallen and preserving the memory of war dead.

This kind of "sacred storytelling" persisted well into the twentieth century. For example, it found its way into a piece published by the *Georgia Review* in the Fall of 1950. The author (presumably white) offered a historical sketch of a Confederate naval expedition "on a dark and rainy night in June 1864," when a Lt. Thomas P. Pelot was able to capture and board the Union gunboat the *Water Witch.* Pelot died in hand-to-hand combat, with comrades fighting by his side. The author described Pelot's tombstone in Laurel Grove Cemetery in Savannah and then testified: "Many years ago a distinguished-looking, heavy-set colored man used to visit his grave every Memorial Day. Tenderly he would lay a wreath upon it, praying the attendants at the Cemetery to tidy up the spot. . . . He was a dignified, unobtrusive man whom everyone addressed as 'Colonel.'"[21] The author identified this mysterious colonel as John H. Deveaux who was "looked upon by the white people of Georgia as a Negro Republican politician" because he had served as collector of customs in Savannah, maintaining the patronage of successive Republican Presidents Harrison, McKinley, Roosevelt and Taft. Deveaux was well known as a "long-time federal office-holder."

The author of Pelot's memorial went on to explain that Deveaux, when queried about tending the fallen Confederate's grave, confessed "I was an enlisted man in the Confederate Navy and had the honor of serving under the brave man buried here." The author adds poetically, "There was a faraway look in his eyes as he added quietly: 'I was with Lieutenant Pelot the night he was killed aboard the *Water Witch.*'"[22]

Both Tom, Cheves McCord's African American valet, and John T. Deveaux, Pelot's surviving black comrade, may indeed have been individuals devoted and attached to the memory of these Confederate "heroes." But what makes these dead whites even more heroic is the role of the "faithful retainer" in these tales. The interracial aspects of this devotion are vital to Confederate legends, a credo to which white Southerners adhered. Both black and white hero worship were essential ingredients of Confederate canonization.

Langdon Cheves McCord's immortality is an achievement earned by the devoted commemorators who exalt him—the sacrifice of his superior life can be redeemed by hallowed consecrations and active penance. The parable of atonement uplifts this fallen hero—and the perpetuation of legendary valor remains the crowning achievement of Confederate patriotism.

With the surrender at Appomattox, many in the white South were given the opportunity to set aside bitterness and rejoin the Union. Smythe confides that although "the oath of allegiance was required as a condition of being able to reclaim property," her mother "*couldn't* take the oath."[23] Louisa Smythe's husband, Augustine, took the oath instead, to reclaim the family homestead at Lang Syne, which, along with other land, Louisa McCord sold to her son-in-law for five dollars.[24]

Taking the oath was one of the most sentimentalized and divisive elements within the postwar era. John Rogers's 1866 statue "Taking the Oath and Drawing Rations" offers a view full of conflict and poignance. As the shamed white child buries his face in his mother's skirts, the Confederate matron averts her eyes while her husband removes his hat to perform the necessary but humiliating ordeal. Meanwhile, the ironic exclamation point is the young, innocent-looking African American, counterposed next to the long-suffering white Confederates. We may not be able to fully understand the mix of emotions, but this portrait of pained surrender is as vivid as Lee's ordeal at Appomattox.

Louisa McCord certainly felt downtrodden. Her daughter's ill health and Augustine Smythe's lack of skills led to the sale of Lang Syne. The Smythes and Louisa McCord established households in Charleston. Louisa McCord remained a bitter opponent of federal authority, devoting her energies to the Lost Cause. In 1870 her patriotic zeal led her into a controversial fight. She decided to resign as president of the South Carolina Monument Association, a group organized to build a memorial to the Confederate dead, rather than continue to work with the Republicans who controlled South Carolina. She offered her reasons for resignation in a letter to the Board of Managers: "A powerful faction in our State, which seeks for her the degradation of negro equality, is forcing itself fearfully forward. . . . Because to our beloved dead, prin-

Taking the Oath and Drawing Rations by John Rogers.
Courtesy of the New York Historical Society,
New York City.

ciples are nobler monument than marble. Because three generations of honored graves that for me, South Carolina bears upon her breast, would become to me a constantly haunting reproach, could I link hands, even in the performance of a good act, with the murderers of her fair fame."[25] Devotion to the memory of her father, her husband, and her son prompted her emotional response.

McCord's dedication to Confederate principles led her into exile, as she pulled up stakes and resettled in Canada. When McCord did return to her beloved South Carolina in 1876, presumably the political tide was turning. Back in her homeland, she dedicated her energies to preparing a biography of her beloved father, a literary tribute left behind in her papers following her death in 1879.

Louisa McCord Smythe had formidable footsteps in which to follow. Subsequent to her mother's death, Louisa Smythe remained devoted to her family of growing children. But in later years, she undertook literary projects, as her mother had before her. Louisa McCord Smythe produced one of the scores of war memoirs that sprang forth at the turn of the century. Again, her Confederate recollections promoted the image of self-sacrifice on the part of the white South and devotion on the part of the black South. Smythe went on to contribute to another heroic volume: *South Carolina Women in the Confederacy,* published in Columbia in 1903. Smythe willingly took on the mantle of historian both to preserve her mother's contributions and to redeem her family's legendary sacrifice: Capt. Langdon Cheves McCord.

While the white South toiled in the fields of neo-Confederate revisionism, those black Southerners who had struggled with the enormous challenges of Reconstruction saw their many gains slipping away. It was a constant tug-of-war of rights and rhetoric in the postwar period. Most black political figures in the South conceded defeat by the turn of the century. However, the generation who seized opportunities in the wake of Confederate surrender provided dramatic examples of pathbreaking and offer testimony that calls us back to re-examine this critical period in South Carolina history.

Again, the story of one remarkable woman, Frances Rollin, and her literary efforts can tell us much about a neglected dimension of legendary valor: the role of the black soldier, those forgotten heroes of the Civil War. But to begin we need to understand Rollin's early years that led her to become one of the staunchest defenders of black rights in postwar South Carolina, and indeed, the biographer of Capt. Martin J. Delany, the only black commissioned officer in the Civil War.

The free black community in Charleston was a small but significant number in antebellum South Carolina. After 1794, some free blacks in Charleston became members of the Brown Fellowship Society, a group that acquired property and maintained a credit union, but most important, created the trappings of aristocracy. By 1860 when war threatened, over one hundred free blacks in Charleston were themselves slaveholders, having acquired nearly four hundred slaves. Many of these black slaveholders were members of the Brown Society. When secession threatened to set the city on fire, members of the mulatto elite took a stand and pledged their loyalty to the state: "In our veins flows the blood of the white race, in some half, in others much more than half white blood. . . . Our allegiance is due to South Carolina and in her defense, we will offer up our lives, and all that is dear to us."[26] This declaration demonstrated their commitment to their communities, to their state, and their willingness to do anything to protect their future stake in South Carolina.

William Rollin was not a member of the Brown Society, but he had the credentials to belong. When mulattos were given their citizenship in 1792 in the French colony of St. Domingue, the commanding officer of the Patriotic Troops of the West, Gen. Jean Baptiste de Caradeuc, resigned his post rather than to endure the prospect of black suffrage. When he left the island for South Carolina, he ironically brought with him his black family, as well as white family members. The de Caradeuc family settled in St. Thomas parish South Carolina with their 188 slaves, including an older black woman known as Vieille Grannie, who was given her own house—perhaps a privilege of concubinage.[27]

William Rollin, a merchant living in Charleston, was connected to the de Caradeucs—if not by blood, then by his extensive business dealings. He had a strong market relationship with the de Caradeuc holdings and was intimately connected with the family. He married Margarette, a light-skinned woman from St. Domingue, in a Catholic ceremony in 1844. The Rollins owned three slaves, making them part of Charleston's brown elite. On November 19, 1845, the oldest of their five daughters, Frances, was born, soon followed by Charlotte, Louisa, Kate, and Florence. Frances and her sisters were given a French education in local private schools.[28] Frances frequently accompanied her father on some of his business trips—to Boston, Philadelphia, Providence, Newport, and even New York.

Rollin had hoped to send his eldest daughter to Paris to finish her education, which was not an unusual ambition for a member of the mulatto class. Instead, in 1859 Frances and three of her sisters were sent to live with the Morris Brown family in Philadelphia where they matriculated at the Quaker Institute for Colored Youth (founded in 1837). Frances Rollin also attended St. Thomas Episcopal, a prominent African Methodist Episcopal Church.

Back in Charleston, William Rollin was hit hard by the war. His business was completely disrupted. Four of his five daughters were stranded in Philadelphia and economic hardship reduced him to farming and selling his goods to Confederate troops to support his family. When Union forces threatened to occupy Charleston, Confederate troops burned railroad depots, warehouses, and finally deserted the city on February 17, 1865, in anticipation of Union invasion. On February 18, the Twenty-first Colored Infantry marched into town, soon joined by the Fifty-fourth Massachusetts and other Union regiments. Rollin was actually wounded defending his land from Union marauders, and the tale of his bravery—in the face of federal soldiers, has been handed down among Rollin descendants.

In 1865 Frances, nicknamed Frank, returned South from Philadelphia. Despite the Confederate sympathies of her family, she was a staunch Unionist, especially in the wake of Confederate defeat. The well educated young woman traveled to Hilton Head and became a teacher, first for the Freedman's Bureau and then for the American Missionary Association—earning fifteen dollars per month.[29] Rollin was crossing to the sea islands on a steamer when she was refused a first class seat by the ferry captain. She decided to lodge a complaint and eventually sue—a most propitious protest, as it put her in contact with Capt. Martin Delany.

Delany was a remarkable figure—a novelist, physician, and political editor before his enlistment in the Union army. He had attended Harvard Medical School, the first black ever to do so. He was a co-founder (with Frederick Douglass) of the *North Star,* and the editor of his own newspaper in Pittsburgh, the *Mystery.* His commission was a remarkable honor, supervised by Lincoln himself. Delany served the army in South Carolina and was eventually attached to the Freedman's Bureau.

Delany encouraged Rollin in her legal action against the sea captain and she eventually won her case; the captain paid a fine of $250. During the proceedings, Delany was impressed with the remarkable young woman, and Rollin confided to him that she wanted to become a writer. Delany then commissioned her to write his life story and promised financial support until she was able to complete the manuscript. He would provide her with enough funds to travel to Boston, undertake research, and complete her authorized biography. Rollin set out for Massachusetts late in the Fall of 1867.

The political and intellectual climate in Massachusetts was stimulating to the talented young black woman. Rollin attended readings by Emerson, Dickens, and Longfellow, among others. She also was welcomed into a circle of black intelligentsia, including Richard T. Greener, the first black graduate of Harvard. She worked hard on her Delany project throughout the Winter of 1867–68.

Ironically, while political events in South Carolina were disturbing to Louisa McCord, they were equally distressing to Frances Rollin—but for very different reasons. Rollin was as disappointed by the slowness of African American political advancement as McCord was chagrined by speed with which South Carolina granted blacks their rights. Rollin wrote in disgust following Washington's Birthday celebration: "If things continue as they are, there will be but little country to celebrate it."[30]

A short time after, in March 1868, Frances Rollin completed a draft of her Delany biography, which was praised by the famed antislavery editor William Lloyd Garrison and sent off by him to Ticknor and Fields on her behalf. The completion of the book did not bring her much peace of mind, as she confessed: "It has been no easy task to me writing under so many difficulties and uncertain of my prospects while it is in the hands of publishers."[31] The rejection that followed from Ticknor and Fields in April was a harsh blow.

By late Spring Delany had withdrawn his financial support and Rollin was forced to sew for pay to support herself. A friend helped her secure work as a copyist for the Massachusetts legislature, but sagging spirits plagued Rollin as Summer approached. She was also worried about her family, as letters from home reported her father's financial worries and her mother's declining health. Rollin's plight prompted the Rev. E. J. Adams of Charleston to recommend the young woman as a clerk to a black lawyer about to assume state office in Columbia. Even though Frances Rollin secured a Boston publisher, Lee and Shepherd, for her life of Delany, she welcomed the return to South Carolina and the prospect of steady employment.

Frances Rollin's book was published in the Fall of 1868 under the title *Life and Public Services of Martin R. Delany.* The title page lists the author as Frank Rollin. A number of nineteenth-century women authors published under a male pseudonym. Rollin's use of her nickname served two purposes—to disguise her gender while preserving her identity.

Frances Anne Rollin was the first black woman historian in America.[32] Rollin's biography is a truly remarkable achievement, especially remarkable considering the obstacles in her path. Rollin was a young black woman from the South writing in the midst of the greatest crucible this country has ever seen. The very fact that she published such a book would be enough to induct her into a pantheon of outstanding scholars. But a close reading of the text reveals both a compelling portrait of Delany and insight into the painful progress of an entire people, the struggle of obtaining full citizenship.

In her introduction, dated October 19, 1868, Rollin offers the grand scope of her project: "We are enabled to look more soberly upon the stupendous revolution, its causes and teachings, and to consider the men and new measures developed through its agency, the material with which the country is to be reconstructed."[33] She wants to place the African American squarely at the center of the war, with a "view of their patriotism and valor in the hour of peril and treachery." She spotlights the enormous sacrifice of black men in blue: "Before the walls of Petersburg, these were among the gallant soldiers who gave battle to the trained veterans of Lee, and at the ramparts of Wagner they waded to victory in blood."[34]

Even more crucial, she highlights the nobility of this contribution because of the excessive and extensive discrimination black soldiers suffered. As Rollin complained: "Of an army of more than a quarter of a million, less than a decade received promotion for their services."[35] The injustice of it all rankles Rollin, but she maintains a celebratory rather than condemnatory tone. Martin Delany is the object of her adoration because of "his singularly active and eventful life, which, in view of the narrow limits apportioned to him, will bear favorable comparison with the great Americans of our time."[36]

Rollin portrays Delany as a race man, as someone who clearly marched to an African drumbeat. She discloses that Frederick Douglass distinguished himself from Delany by confessing, "I thank God for making me a man simply, but Delany always thanks Him for making him a *black man.*"[37] She points out that just as statesman John Randolph of

Frances Rollin Whipper.
Courtesy of Ione.

Roanoke boasted of his Indian ancestry, so Virginian Martin Delany took pride in his descent from the Mandingoes and other African ancestors.

Perhaps it was only fitting that someone with such an uncompromising pride in his color would be granted the glory of being the only black commissioned as an officer by the Union government.[38] Rollin's biography provides a step-by-step analysis of the greatness Delany achieved at each juncture of his career: leaving Virginia for opportunity in Pittsburgh, studying medicine, editing a newspaper, exiling himself to Canada, and other emblematic gestures.

Within Rollin's framework, all roads led to the crucial role for which Delany was destined. In the midst of crisis, he applied to be a surgeon in the army, to serve with black troops. His first offer was ignored, but finally Delany was interviewed by Lincoln himself—then offered his commission directly from the office of the Secretary of War in February 1865.

Once anointed, responsibilities weighed heavily, as Ben Wade, president of the Senate confided to Delany: "You are the first of your race who has been thus honored by the government; therefore much depends and will be expected of you."[39] Delany went to South Carolina, assigned to Gen. Rufus Saxton. In Charleston, preparing for the celebration to raise the United States flag again over Ft. Sumter, Delany proposed that he recruit and train an Armée d'Afrique, a corps of black officers and black soldiers.[40]

Although Confederate surrender and peace interrupted this ambitious plan, Delany continued his work on behalf of his people at his post in Hilton Head. When he was offered the principalship of a freedpeople's school, he declined in favor of practicing medicine. But Delany was willing to take charge until a suitable replacement could be found. He proved a revolutionary educator: "The rules laid down by the board allowed *whipping*, while they forbade suspension or dismissal of the pupils from school. To flog a pupil, he alleged, was an evidence of the incapacity for governing on the part of the teacher and that when it was evident a pupil could not be restrained without resorting to such measures, he was unfit to be among the others."[41] Perhaps these views, and Delany's advanced theories on female education, converted Rollin into one of his disciples: "He argued that 'men were never raised in social position above the level of women; therefore men could not be elevated without women's elevation; further, that among the nations of the world where women were kept in ignorance, great philosophers, or statesmen failed to be produced, as a general rule.'"[42] Rollin remained a loyal and devoted convert, a biographer worthy of her subject.

Rollin and her generation knew the surrender of the Confederate government created unprecedented opportunity for transformation. Delany himself proposed the "Triple Alliance" of capital from the North, land from the former planters and labor from the former slaves. Rollin's book was a rallying cry, as she closed the volume with stirring sentiment:

> The late revolution has resulted in bringing the race to which he belongs into prominence. They have begun their onwards march towards that higher civilization promised at the close of the war. Let no unhallowed voice be lifted to stay their progress; then, with all barriers removed, the glorious destiny promised to them can be achieved. And then our country, continuing to recognize merit alone in the children, as shown in the appointment of the black major of Carolina, will add renewed strength to her greatness. Begirt with loyal hearts and strong arms, the mission of our revolution shall embrace centuries in its march, securing the future stability of our country, and proclaiming with truthfulness the grandeur of republican institutions to the civilization of Christendom.[43]

Indeed, in 1868, Frances Rollin embraced her own role in this grand scheme of things.

Securing a publisher for her book, Rollin returned to South Carolina to clerk for William J. Whipper, a northern black lawyer, who represented Hilton Head in the state legislature. Whipper was a widower with a one-year-old son, Buddy, and an adopted son, Demps Powell, who had attached himself to Whipper during army days. Whipper was a flamboyant and charismatic figure, who charmed his way into Frances Rollin's heart. Rollin had been courted by many during her Boston sojourn, but it was the man dismissed by her family as "nothing but a country lawyer" who won her hand.[44] Their whirlwind courtship took perhaps even Rollin by surprise, as Whipper picked her up in his buggy at the train depot in Columbia on August 2, and by August 14 he had proposed.

Whipper was an eloquent speaker on behalf of black rights and had even championed women during a speech at the South Carolina constitutional convention:

> However frivolous you may think it, I think the time will come when every man and woman in this country will have the right to vote. I acknowledge the superiority of women. There are large numbers of the sex who have an intelligence more than equal to our own. Is it right or just to deprive these intelligent beings of the privileges which we enjoy? The time will come when you will have to answer this question. It will continue to be agitated until it must ultimately triumph. However derisively we may treat these noble women who are struggling for their sex, we shall yet see them successful in the assertion of their rights.[45]

Unfortunately, Whipper's attempt to have the word "male" struck from the election law failed.

Rollin was drawn to this ambitious and simpatico figure. She later hinted at the key to their partnership when she confessed: "It is proper here to say Mr. Whipper possessed the necessary ability and courage to command any honor in the gift of his party [Republican], while his wife had all the ambition, zeal and bravery to urge him to the front."[46] Clerking with him on the Judiciary Committee of South Carolina must have seemed like the front lines, as the two struggled side by side. Despite the objections of her family and any lingering doubts, Rollin consented to the marriage on August 22 and the two were married the next month.

The couple had a tumultuous relationship. Frances Whipper bore five children, one died in infancy and another died when only a year old. But her three surviving children, daughters Winifred and Iona and son Leigh, provided focus for Frances Whipper, and each of her children testified to her vision and sense of achievement. William Whipper's gambling and drinking problems plagued the family, but Frank seemed to be the center and force that held together the Whipper household. Frances Whipper ran her husband's Beaufort newspaper during his frequent absences.

In 1880 Frank took her three children and relocated to Washington where she secured a job as a copyist in the federal Land Office. William Whipper joined the family in 1882, but returned to South Carolina in 1885 to serve as a probate judge. As a result of his patronage appointment, Frances Whipper was singled out for political reprisal and lost her government position. She was rescued by an admirer, Frederick Douglass, recorder of deeds for the District of Columbia, who offered Frank work—and was perhaps aware of the rumors that Whipper had taken up with another woman back in Beaufort. In 1889 Frank returned to South Carolina with her daughter where she died in 1901. The Whippers apparently never reconciled, and their dream of social revolution remained unfulfilled.

Indeed, just as Frances Rollin Whipper returned to South Carolina, the decade that has been called the nadir of American race relations descended. The gains of Emancipation and constitutional amendments were diminished by the ascendancy of Jim Crow, crowned in 1896 with the Supreme Court's *Plessy v. Ferguson* ruling.

The postwar generation of black politicians was under siege—Whipper himself was imprisoned in 1888 when he refused to cede office following a rigged election. He served thirteen months in jail before giving up his protest. The rise of terrorist violence was perhaps the most marked change of the 1890s, as lynchers seized on victims at least four times a month at the opening of the decade, increasing to an average of three deaths per week by 1894. The hopes of Frances Rollin Whipper were being destroyed by bands waving torches—as blood drenched the soil of her home state of South Carolina.

This era of racial retribution set the stage for the apologist neo-Confederate literature that poured forth at the turn of the century. While the Confederate dead could never be brought back to life, immortality might be achieved if antebellum values of white supremacy were maintained. Thus both Louisa McCord's uncompromising stance and her son's sacrifice were embalmed and enhanced by Louisa McCord Smythe's memorial, *For Old Lang Syne,* while Rollin's *Life and Public Services of Martin R. Delany* went out of print.

The dueling ideologies of Smythe and Rollin are both preserved for us today—to ponder, to reflect, and to renew our appreciation of the compelling complexity of Civil War stories. The legendary valor that I propose we celebrate includes the accomplishments of these two remarkable South Carolina women whose witness and testimony allow us to puzzle together the southern past.

NOTES

One. Sister against Sister

1. James Henry Gooding, *On the Altar of Freedom: A Black Soldier's Civil War Letters from the Front,* ed. Virginia M. Adams (Amherst: University of Massachusetts Press, 1991).

2. Lauren Cook Burgess, *An Uncommon Soldier* (New York: Oxford University Press, 1995).

3. See Mark Grimsley, *The Hard Hand of War* (New York: Cambridge University Press, 1995).

4. See for example LeeAnn Whites, *The Civil War as a Crisis in Gender* (Athens: University of Georgia Press, 1995); Drew Gilpin Faust, *Mothers of Invention* (Chapel Hill: University of North Carolina Press, 1996).

5. I will depend heavily on the work of previous scholars, most notably Malcolm Bell, whose splendid volume *Major Butler's Legacy: Five Generations of a Slaveholding Family* (Athens: University of Georgia Press, 1987) has proved invaluable to my ongoing work on Kemble. When Mary Lynn Pedersen contacted me and arrived in Boston seeking assistance for her master's essay on Kemble, I offered her books, copies of manuscript material, and transcriptions of letters from my ongoing work on Fanny Kemble. She incorporated them into her very thoughtful master's essay, "Sister against Sister: The Story of Sarah and Frances Butler and Their Ideological Split During the War" (M.A., University of Georgia, 1992), and I was flattered when she borrowed my working title as well.

6. For an expanded treatment, see Catherine Clinton, *Fanny Kemble's Civil Wars* (forthcoming).

7. Frances Anne Kemble, *Journal of Residence in America,* vol. 2 (London: John Murray, 1835), p. 82.

8. Kemble, *Journal,* p. 255. This description is laden with irony in

that when Kemble married and settled in Philadelphia she found its dullness oppressive.

9. Margaret Armstrong, *Fanny Kemble* (New York: MacMillan, 1938), p. 176.

10. Frances Anne Kemble, *Records of Girlhood,* vol. 3 (New York: Henry Holt & Co., 1879), p. 320.

11. Fanny Kemble Wister, *Fanny, the American Kemble* (Tallahassee, Fla.: South Pass Press, 1972), p. 140.

12. Frances Anne Kemble to Katherine Sedgwick, May 31, 1834, Sedgwick Collection, Massachusetts Historical Society.

13. Frances Anne Kemble, *Records of Later Life* (New York: Henry Holt & Co., 1882), p. 2.

14. Pierce Butler, *Mr. Butler's Statement* (Philadelphia: privately published, 1850), p. 25.

15. Kemble, *Records of Later Life,* p. 41.

16. Ibid., p. 31.

17. See Catherine Clinton, "Maria Weston Chapman," in *Portraits of American Women,* ed. G. J. Barker-Benfield and Catherine Clinton (New York: Oxford University Press, 1998).

18. See Pierce Butler Letterbook, 1851. Pierce Butler to Harriet St. Leger, August 20, 1851, Wister Family Collection, Historical Society of Pennsylvania (HSP).

19. Diary of Sidney George Fisher, June 3, 1856: "Heard from Henry that Butler has well nigh ruined his splendid estate by stock gambling." Nicholas B. Wainwright, ed., *A Philadelphia Perspective: The Diary of Sidney George Fisher Covering the Years 1834–7* (Philadelphia: Historical Society of Pennsylvania, 1967), p. 257.

20. Bell, *Major Butler's Legacy,* p. 476.

21. John L. Cobb, *Owen Wister* (Boston: Twayne Publishers, 1984), p. 2.

22. The witty and observant Sidney George Fisher confided to his diary on August 27, 1860: "Pay a visit to Mrs. Kemble at Dr. Wister's. Saw her & Mrs. Wister & spent a very pleasant evening with them.

Always liked Mrs. Kemble. She is a woman of genius & of noble impulses & kind feelings. Too much will & vitality & force of character, to be very happy in domestic life, more especially with such a man as Butler, her inferior far in all intellectual endowments, but her equal in firmness & strength of character. She is not a person to be governed by force. They could not live together and, after much unhappiness, were divorced. Her manners & conversation this evening more quiet than they used to be and she was very cordial and easy & pleasant." Wainwright, *Philadelphia Perspective,* p. 360.

23. Sarah Butler Wister to FAK, February 5, 1865, Wister Family Collection, HSP.

24. Frances Butler Leigh, *Ten Years on a Georgia Plantation since the War* (London: R. Bentley, 1883).

25. Wainwright, *Philadelphia Perspective,* Fisher Diary, December 26, 1860, p. 375.

26. Fanny Kemble Wister, ed. "Sarah B. Wister's Civil War Diary," *Pennsylvania Magazine of History and Biography,* vol. 52, July 1978, p. 304.

27. Wister, ed., "Diary," p. 275.

28. Wister, ed., "Diary," p. 297. Later in the diary she makes a sarcastic observation: "The root of all American patriotism is state feeling, that the only love or pride of country they acknowledge. Probably my lack of nationality is oweing to the impossibility of getting up a pride in Pennsylvania." June 5, 1861, p. 304.

29. Wister, ed., "Diary," April 21, 1861, p. 281.

30. Wister, ed., "Diary," April 26, 1861, p. 289.

31. Wister, ed., "Diary," May 28, 1861, p. 302.

32. Wister, ed., "Diary."

33. Wister, ed., "Diary," July 13, 1861, p. 315.

34. Wister, ed., "Diary," August 20, 1861, p. 322.

35. Frances Anne Kemble, *Further Records* (New York: Henry Holt & Co., 1891), p. 335.

36. Wister, ed. "Diary," August 24, 1861, p. 324.

37. He also reported that Fan's activities were becoming the subject of speculation, and Sarah would have to talk to her sister about behaving more discreetly. Owen Wister to Sarah Wister, August 31, 1861, box 8, Wister Family Collection, HSP. Surprisingly, on September 5, Sarah tells Owen she will not cut her visit short because she and her mother are getting along so well.

38. Bell, *Major Butler's Legacy,* p. 350.

39. June 6, 1863.

40. J. C. Furnas, *Fanny Kemble: Leading Lady of the Nineteenth Century Stage* (New York: Dial Press, 1982), p. 406.

41. Leigh, *Ten Years,* p. 14.

42. Sarah Wister to Owen Wister, April 30, 1867, Wister Family Collection, HSP.

43. Ibid.

44. Bell, *Major Butler's Legacy,* p. 398.

45. Bell, *Major Butler's Legacy,* p. 401.

46. Sarah Wister to Owen Wister, November 28, 1867, Wister Family Collection, HSP.

47. Leigh, *Ten Years,* p. 133.

48. Leigh, *Ten Years,* p. 201.

49. Sarah Wister, "The Early Years of a Child of Promise," Wister Family Collection, HSP.

50. Sarah Butler Wister to Fanny Butler Leigh, December 17, 1880, Wister Family Collection, HSP.

51. Both girls were doubtless profoundly affected by Fanny Kemble's phobia about inherited mental disease. Kemble's mother, brother, and nephew all suffered mental disorders, and her brother died in an institution.

52. Furnas, *Fanny Kemble,* p. 414.

53. Fanny Butler Leigh to Frances Anne Kemble, May 1, 1881 and response, box 1, folder 8, Wister Family Collection, HSP.

54. Ibid.

55. Leigh, *Ten Years,* p. 230–37.

56. Bell, *Major Butler's Legacy,* p. 447.

57. See Martin H. Greenberg, Charles Waugh, and Frank D. McSherry, eds., *Civil War Women II,* (Little Rock: August House Publishing, 1997).

58. Malcolm Bell offers splendid insight into the controversy over Wister's novel, *Lady Baltimore,* when none other than Teddy Roosevelt, Wister's Harvard classmate, took him to task for his neo-Confederate views.

Two. Orphans of the Storm

1. There are several ongoing projects being researched on children and the Civil War. Peter Bardaglio's excellent essay, "The Children of Jubilee: African American Childhood in Wartime," in *Divided Houses: Gender and the Civil War,* ed. Catherine Clinton and Nina Silber (New York: Oxford University Press, 1992), is a harbinger of things to come. Also James Marten's "Fatherhood in the Confederacy: Southern Soldiers and Their Children," in *Journal of Southern History,* vol. 63, no. 2, May 1997, will be incorporated into his larger work *No Medals, No Monuments: The Children's Civil War* (Chapel Hill: University of North Carolina, in press). Marten's book will include a section on orphans and orphanages in his final chapter. Lee Drago of the College of Charleston is undertaking a project on Confederate children.

2. Judith Dalberger, *Mother Donit Fore the Best: Correspondence of a Nineteenth Century Orphan Asylum* (Syracuse: Syracuse University Press, 1996).

3. Joan Brady, *Theory of War* (New York: Knopf, 1993).

4. After the war, the expansion of Catholic orphanages, charity hospitals, and other institutions was inevitable. They became more fully integrated into their secular communities. In Charleston, the Sisters of Our Lady of Mercy were supported by prominent non-Catholic legislators, as they petitioned to obtain state funding to con-

tinue their institutional work. See "Speech of the Hon. C. C. Brown," March 21, 1870, Caroliniana Collection, University of South Carolina, Columbia.

5. Harry Giovannoli, *Kentucky Female Orphan School: A History* (n. p.: Midway, Kentucky, 1930), p. 66.

6. Giovannoli, *Orphan School,* p. 69.

7. *The Orphan's Appeal,* Palmetto Orphan Home, Columbia, S.C., May 1873.

8. *Charleston Daily Courier,* September 22, 1865.

9. *The Orphan's Appeal,* December 1873.

10. *The Orphan's Appeal,* March and May 1873.

11. "*Ceremonies at the Reception of the Orphan Children of Pennsylvania Soldiers who Perish Defending the Government by the Governor and the Legislature in the State Capitol: March 16, 1866* (Harrisburg: George Bergner, 1866), p. 10.

12. *Ceremonies,* p. 19.

13. *Ceremonies,* p. 23.

14. A distortion along the lines of saying that the statement: "I'm going on a diet" can be interpreted as "I am getting thinner."

15. (Cambridge: Harvard University Press, 1992).

16. James Laughery Paul, *Pennsylvania's Soldiers' Orphan Schools* (Philadelphia: Claxton, Remsen & Haffelfinger, 1876), p. 439.

17. Paul, *Pennsylvania's Soldiers' Orphan Schools,* p. 441.

18. Paul, *Pennsylvania's Soldiers' Orphan Schools,* p. 146.

19. I am wholly dependent upon and deeply grateful for the scholarship of Kathleen Collins. All quotes and information included in the section on the American Missionary Association portraits are taken from her excellent article: "Portraits of Slave Children," *History of Photography,* July-September, 1985, p. 187–210.

20. The black and white images of these children seem a faint and somewhat creepy historical precedent for images that emerged during the media focus in 1997 (due to the tragic murder of a child in Colorado) on young girls in full make-up and lavish costumes who enter beauty contests.

21. See Gerda Lerner, *The Grimké Sisters from South Carolina*, pp. 359–68. See also Pauli Murray's family memoir, which includes her grandmother Cornelia's story in *Proud Shoes* (New York: Harper & Row, 1978).

22. Lerner, *Grimké Sisters*, p. 359–61.

23. See Janet Hermann, *Pursuit of a Dream* (New York: Oxford University Press, 1981).

24. See, for example, Ira Berlin and Leslie Rowland, eds., *Families and Freedom* (New York: New Press, 1997).

25. Michael Johnson has undertaken a project to explore the reunification of black families after the Civil War.

26. (New York: Free Press, 1994).

27. Office of the Adjutant General Enlisted Branch (OAGEB), box 22, HBE #160, National Archives.

28. OAGEB, box 22, HBE #224, National Archives.

29. OAGEB, box 22, HBE #143, National Archives.

30. Ishbel Ross, *Rebel Rose: Life of Rose O'Neal Greenhow, Confederate Spy* (New York: Ballantine Books, 1973), p. 126.

31. Mary Massey, *Bonnet Brigades: American Women in the Civil War* (New York: Knopf, 1966), p. 91.

32. Rose Greenhow, *My Imprisonment and the First Year of Abolition Rule at Washington* (London: Richard Bentley, 1863), p. 119.

33. Greenhow, *Imprisonment*, p. 133.

34. Greenhow, *Imprisonment*, p. 202–3.

35. Greenhow, *Imprisonment*, p. 217, 243.

36. Ross, *Rebel Rose*, p. 192.

37. Greenhow, *Imprisonment*, p. 303–4.

38. Ross, *Rebel Rose*, p. 235.

39. Ross, *Rebel Rose*, p. 214.

40. Belle Boyd went on stage after her wartime career as a spy. The public had an interest in women whose names were associated with wartime espionage.

41. And we look forward to the work of James Marten, Peter

Bardaglio, Lee Drago, and others to help us put this incredible sacrifice into perspective.

Three. Legendary Valor

1. See, for example, Louisa McCord, *Political and Social Essays*, ed. Richard C. Lounsbury (Charlottesville: University of Virginia, 1995).

2. Louisa McCord Smythe, "Recollections of Louisa McCord Smythe," p. 18. South Carolina Historical Society, Charleston.

3. Carmel Chapline, "'A Tragedy in Five Acts:' The Life of Louisa S. McCord, 1810–1879," M.A. College of Charleston, 1992, p. 135.

4. Eliza Ripley, *Social Life in Old New Orleans: Being Recollections of My Girlhood* (New York: D. Appleton, 1912), p. 210.

5. Smythe, "Recollections," p. 1.

6. Smythe, "Recollections," p. 4.

7. Smythe, "Recollections," p. 67.

8. Smythe, "Recollections," p. 79.

9. Smythe, "Recollections."

10. Smythe, "Recollections."

11. Smythe, "Recollections," p. 55.

12. Smythe, "Recollections," p. 68.

13. Smythe, "Recollections," p. 52.

14. Smythe, "Recollections."

15. Smythe, "Recollections," p. 57.

16. Smythe, "Recollections," p. 58.

17. Smythe, "Recollections."

18. Smythe, "Recollections."

19. Chapline, "Tragedy," M.A. College of Charleston, 1992, p. 138.

20. Smythe, "Recollections," p. 60.

21. Alexander Lawrence, "The Night Lieutenant Pelot Was Killed Aboard the *Water Witch*," *Georgia Review*, Fall 1950, p. 175.

22. Lawrence, "Night," p. 176.

23. Smythe, "Recollections," p. 84.

24. McCord later was persuaded by Dr. Reynolds, her daughter-in-law's father, to take the oath so she could dispose of her property in Columbia—providing for her family rather than risking confiscation.

25. Chapline, "Tragedy," p. 162.

26. Bernard Powers Jr. *Black Charlestonians: A Social History 1822–1885* (Fayetteville: University of Arkansas Press, 1994), p. 65–66.

27. She was perhaps a concubine of her owner, as research by a Rollin descendent supports. When James Achille De Caradeuc died in January 1895, he was identified as a "nephew" of William Rollin—as Marie Augustine, James's mother, was William Rollin's half-sister. See Carol Ione, *Pride of Family: Four Generations of American Women of Color* (New York: Simon & Schuster, 1991).

28. Other free black children from Savannah and Augusta attended these schools in Charleston as well.

29. She befriended Charlotte Forten during this period, whose diary of her sea island stay is a classic wartime journal. See Charlotte Forten Grimké, *The Journals of Charlotte Forten Grimké*, ed. Brenda Stevenson (New York: Oxford University Press, 1991).

30. "The 1868 Diary of Frances Anne Rollin," possession of Ione, p. 17. The author wishes to express her thanks for Ione's generosity and collegiality. She opened her home, her files, and offered invaluable insight while working on this project.

31. "Diary of Rollin," p. 20.

32. Rollin's unpublished diary of 1868 is also a splendid historical document, which I hope Ione will edit and publish soon so that a wider audience can appreciate fully her extraordinary talents.

33. Frank A. Rollin, *Life and Public Services of Martin R. Delany* (Boston: Lee and Shepard, 1868), p. 7.

34. Rollin, *Life and Public*, p. 33.

35. Rollin, *Life and Public*, p. 9. This is only a slight exaggeration, as roughly 180,000 African Americans served in the army, and perhaps another 30,000 in the United States Navy.

36. Rollin, *Life and Public*, p. 11.

37. Rollin, *Life and Public,* p. 19.

38. Rollin, *Life and Public,* p. 40. Rollin makes a vivid juxtaposition of images when she describes Delany's response to a slave rebellion: "With the scene of Nat Turner's defeat and execution before him, he consecrated himself to freedom; and like another Hannibal, registered his vow against the enemies of his race."

39. Rollin, *Life and Public,* p. 177.

40. Rollin, *Life and Public,* p. 193.

41. Rollin, *Life and Public,* p. 289.

42. Rollin, *Life and Public,* p. 49–50.

43. Rollin, *Life and Public,* p. 301.

44. "Nothing but a country lawyer" from conversations with Ione, March 9, 1996. For Frances Rollin's courtship, see Ione, *Pride of Family,* p. 108–12.

45. Ione, *Pride of Family,* p. 166.

46. Frances Rollin Whipper Papers, in possession of Ione.

INDEX